Introduction to

Spiritual Harmony

Introduction to

Spiritual Harmony

By
Jerry Stocking

To correspond with Jerry Stocking
or to find out about other products offered by
Moose Ear Press or A Choice Experience, Inc.
see the last five pages of this book.

Editor: Jackie Stocking
Copy Editor: Roger Anderson
Proofreader: Karen Bates
Cover design and art work: Jerry Stocking

A special thank you to Dan Millman for his timely
telephone call and his useful commentary.

Thank you to all of the people who read the manuscript
or aided in the production of
Introduction to Spiritual Harmony.

Published by
Moose Ear Press
First Printing 1994

ISBN: 0-9629593-1-6

Table of Contents

Dedication

This book is dedicated to the philosopher in each of us because it is the very exploration and development of that philosopher which provides us with our only evolutionary edge.

Introduction

Imagine that you are sitting across from God. You are very much alive and have the opportunity to ask five questions. What would you ask? Rather than interacting with this scenario as theoretical, pretend that it is real — and let the revelations begin!

Introduction to Spiritual Harmony is quick and easy reading. It is a dialogue that can be **read in an evening** and re-read many times. The book is both simple and truthful. In the conversation, flexibility and the importance of amusement and playfulness is valued over the seriousness which is currently robbing us of **thoroughly wonderful lives**. The dialogue is between two characters, a person and God, who explore the human condition together. God is representative of the inspired bliss that exists in all of us. The person takes on the role of being truly ignorant, sometimes embarrassing, always sincere and continually willing to learn.

While I have a background in psychology, philosophy, neuro-linguistic programming and sales, I do not claim to be God or know God's response to your questions, my research for this book revealed a fascinating discovery. The precise questions you would ask God (if you found yourself in His or Her presence) uncovers a story about **you,** reveals problems and unlocks the door to a life filled with **childlike simplicity, warmth, ease and curiosity**. Many people have reported that the process of thinking of their five questions for God was a revelation in itself. *Introduction to Spiritual Harmony* explores possible answers to many commonly asked questions. What are your five questions for God? The answers to your questions may be waiting for you in this book.

What would life be like if you could celebrate and delight in waking, breathing, moving and thinking? How would life be if you could celebrate everything?

The purpose of the dialogue in this book is to make you a better philosopher and to playfully bring into question basic assumptions of life. *Introduction to Spiritual Harmony* provides an opening for living outside the tangle of importance we are often caught in. The main tools used to do this are paradox and contradiction. When we pass on the lessons of life, we pass on the certainty of having them repeated. A bowl of cherries does have pits, but these pits can grow into an orchard of cherry trees.

*****

At thirteen I bought a puzzle ring for $8.00 which, at the time, seemed like a lot of money to me. Upon its purchase, the puzzle was solved and the ring was intact. In the inevitable event that I should take the ring apart, the manufacturers included an index card with instructions on how to solve the puzzle and put the ring back together. After several days I took the ring apart. With the confidence of a person who has the right instructions, I started to put the ring back together. After several frustrating, puzzling hours my ring still did not resemble a ring, and I was both angry and upset. I read the instructions over and over, but I just couldn't solve the puzzle. My $8.00 investment seemed like a big mistake.

At wits end, I showed the instructions and jumbled mess to a friend of mine. To put it bluntly, this friend was not as smart as I was. I had ample evidence to support this assertion ranging from school grades to peer consensus. My friend looked at the instructions and converted the jumbled silver mess into a ring in less than a minute. He then taught me how to put the ring together by doing exactly what the instructions described. His trick was simply to follow the instructions without adding anything to them. Rather than following the instructions, I had attempted to figure them out and had made them much more complicated than they were. Putting the ring together was a simple task made difficult only by adding my own complexity.

With practice, I was soon putting the ring together and taking it apart in less than a minute. Learning to assemble the ring, I developed a newfound respect for my friend and his abilities in practical matters.

As you read this book, I suggest that you read it like my friend read the instructions to the ring. **Read the words without trying to figure them out. Read the book without adding your own complexity.** This may not be easy because we have been taught that big questions require complex answers — they don't. There is nothing for you to figure out in this book and nothing for you to fill in. Read the words that are here and notice the changes that happen in your body, mind and perspective. Above all, **enjoy reading it,** and if the book gets complicated for you, go back to reading the words on the page and stop trying to figure them out. Relax and read on. **Simply read the book and read the book simply.**

The more often you read *Introduction to Spiritual Harmony,* the more useful it will be for you. When you have read this book several times, move on to the book *Spiritual Harmony*, which explores people, reality, spirit, spirituality and the possibilities therein. If you find anything in this book interesting, thought provoking, funny, boring or threatening, you will find *Spiritual Harmony* very rewarding, entertaining and exciting. The purpose of both *Introduction to Spiritual Harmony* and its companion volume, *Spiritual Harmony,* is to bring out the philosopher in each of us and to continually present the opportunity to increase joy and pleasure while moving us toward the kind of curiosity, wonder and confidence that are so much a part of us **at our best.**

1

Emily was born on September 7, 1987 — Labor Day. At her birth I learned more about the beauty of life, love, caring and being human than I had ever known. Like most humans, I was not really present at my own birth — at least the "I" that I define myself as today. At my birth I was Earth — all life — all possibility. I was complete and whole beginning a journey and probably ending some other journey. At Emily's birth I was there watching and participating. I was born myself.

My relationship with my wife rose to new heights during labor. I cannot describe the feelings of watching Emily emerge, but I have relived the feelings and emotions many times. There just aren't words to express the intensity and delight of that eventful day for me. The birth of my son, Judson, five years earlier provided me with the life-changing transition from man to father and altered my very being, which I have since discovered was only a beginning. At Emily's birth my curiosity and love for all human beings expanded into whole new terrain.

My story begins when Emily was three days old and began speaking in complete sentences. Emily wasn't really talking. It was the wisdom of the universe speaking with simplicity and accuracy beyond anything I imagined possible and me hearing it through her innocent presence. This wisdom did not come from Emily's mouth; its source was indistinguishable but could be heard in my ears with more resonating clarity than any sound I had heard before. The voice was neither male or female — high or low. For the sake of my story, I will call the voice God. God spoke with a familiarity and a compassion I had never experienced before.

Emily's personality would develop later, and she would have no recollection of these dialogues. Their effect on her is apparent to me, however, every time I look into her pure trusting eyes and see her relaxed, easy and frequent smiles. But I am getting ahead of myself. Emily was three days old and asleep in her crib the evening that I first heard from God....

God: Is there anything you would like to know?

Me: Who are you?

God: I am your daughter and yet not your daughter.

Me: What do you mean by that?

God: I am speaking through your daughter, but I am not

limited to her, nor is she limited to me. Your daughter will develop her own unique personality as she grows and matures. There is, however, a period here before her consciousness arrives where she and I are obviously one. During this period you and I will speak from time to time. At some point your daughter will develop her own world and I will only speak through her being as I do with everyone else.

Me: I don't quite understand. Are you God?

God: Yes.

Me: And I can just talk with you about anything I wish?

God: Yes. Is there anything you want?

Me: I don't really want anything.

God: Nothing?

Me: Well, I do have a few questions I would like answered.

God: What are your questions?

Me: First of all, what is the purpose of life?

God: That I have left up to you. What is the purpose of life?

Me: I don't know—that is why I asked.

God: That is one of those questions that, if I were you, I would answer soon. That way you would have some idea of what you are doing or even why you are doing it. It is an important question and I suggest you answer it often.

Me: Do You have any hints for me?

God: Yes. I gave you everything you need to make up a purpose. And, you already live with a purpose. That purpose is evident and obvious in everything you do. Look at yourself and your life. These are some of the obvious results of your purpose. Now determine whether or not you like the results. If you do, keep the purpose, and if not, change it.

Me: My purpose doesn't look obvious to me.

God: So your first purpose is to find out what your purpose is, and the second one is to determine whether you want that to be your purpose. Are you having any fun yet?

Me: Do you mean am I having fun in this conversation or am I having any fun in my life?

God: What is the difference?

Me: I get Your point. But it can't really matter to You whether I am having fun. I mean, is the Pope having fun?

God: Who? It's accurate to say that I don't care if you are having fun, **but you do care.** It seems that one of the things I constantly hear from people on Earth is that they want to have fun or that they want things to be better than they are. Usually they call on me because they have come up with some new answer to what they need in order for life to be more fun and rewarding. That is why I originally asked you what you wanted. I keep getting requests from people on Earth for all kinds of things (a pony, a new car, tennis shoes) none of which I keep in inventory. **If you can't be perfectly content with nothing, you obviously can't be content with anything.** At birth, I gave you everything you need to be happy and to have a meaningful, rewarding life. If you needed a new car or a new house, I would have given them to you at birth. I didn't, and nothing that you add after birth has any chance of succeeding in having your life be more important or rewarding. The moment you focus on anything that you did not have at birth, you are buying the line that you are somehow incomplete and can be fulfilled from outside yourself. This sort of approach is never going to work very well and may ultimately result in the end of your species. What you had at birth is what you need, nothing more and nothing less.

Me: You mean I already have everything I need?

God: Yes. Not only do you already have everything you need — you always did.

Me: That is easy for You to say.

God: That is true.

Me: Do You mean that I shouldn't buy that new car I have been saving for?

God: No. I never said that you shouldn't buy it. If you expect it to contribute to the quality of your life or if you expect things to get better when you get it, then you will end up being disappointed. Personally, I don't care if you buy the car. It makes no difference to me. If it makes a difference to you, then you are making something important that I don't make important, which puts you on some pretty shaky ground.

Me: You mean that I should make important the same things You make important?

God: It wouldn't hurt. You could do worse than using me as a model. If you doubt that, look around you.

Me: What do You make important?

God: That is something for you to discover.

Me: That sounds like it could be an interesting purpose: to find out what is important to God and then have those same things be important to me.

God: That makes sense to me, though I suspect that you might make a big mistake in how you go about it. People have continually attempted to determine what is important to me by looking through their eyes. This process results in looking at the infinite in a short-sighted way. When people do this, they don't see the infinite — they see a little of the infinite and think that it is infinite. This sort of approach has allowed people to fight, kill and love in my name. I do not take sides and never have; if it looks like I do, that is the part you add. Since you will be looking at me with your eyes, you cannot see me, so you might just as well look at yourself. After all, you are not some accident. I gave you everything you need at birth, so all of your answers, questions and roots of satisfaction are within you. Look at yourself and you will find me.

Me: Thanks for that. Can I ask a different question?

God: Yes.

Me: What am I to do?

God: I can't understand why you would do anything but go ahead if you want to. I put you in paradise and thus far you have been expending mass quantities of effort attempting to improve on it. You build cities, and then you have to build parks. **The whole Earth is a park with enough variation to be interesting and enough similarity to be familiar.** It amazes me that you think you can improve on my creation. Good luck. Remember that you had everything you needed at birth; everything else comes after birth. People have made "after-birth" into an industry, many industries. There is nothing for you to do.

Me: But I have to do something; otherwise, what is the point in being alive?

God: Exactly, what is the point in being alive?

Me: I didn't ask the question for You to agree with me. I was hoping that You would give me the answer.

God: I am always giving you the answer, but you don't hear it. I can't help but give you the answer even though I don't think it is a good idea to do so. I am an open book, and the answer is right here anytime, all the time.

Me: Is the open book the Bible?

God: Sorry, I haven't read it, so I am hardly qualified to discuss it. I can, however, tell you I have never seen the same book interpreted so many different ways by so many different people. I plan on reading the Bible some day, but I am a little afraid of it. People have used that little black book to justify so many things.

Me: You have not read the Bible?

God: That's right. If you had observed a group of people turn paradise into a living hell or a hollow shell, would you want to read the book most of those people were reading? Isn't it obvious that somewhere you are finding justification for the silliness people are so occupied with? I suspect that when I read your Bible, I will discover that it doesn't really say anything or that it says everything and that either way, it can be interpreted to mean anything. It can result in the feeding of peasants one minute and the killing of them the next. It never ceases to amaze me that people can think they know me, try to improve on my creation or ignore me altogether. What you miss is that on Earth everything you need to know is obvious. Your surroundings and your appreciation and respect for your surroundings indicate how you are doing and how you should live. I arranged for you to populate Earth so that if you ever got confused within yourself, you could look outside yourself and observe your effect on others to know how you are doing. I have not yet figured out how to make a simpler, more obvious place than Earth. I did the best I could and people don't get it. Sometimes I wonder how many times you will stumble over the obvious before you see it. You seem so intent on confusion. The more time you have, the more complex you make things. There is nothing particularly complicated on Earth. Everything is as simple and obvious as it could possibly be.

Me: You mean what we have here, life on Earth, is easy?

God: Yes.

Me: I still don't know what to do. You said it was all right to buy a new car, but how should I raise my children?

God: I didn't say it was all right to buy the new car. I said that it doesn't matter. It seems that even in your conversations with me you misinterpret what I have said. The next thing you might do is say that God told you to buy a new car. I didn't tell you to buy it or not to buy it. Buy it if you buy it, and don't if you don't. That is part of the simplicity of Earth. Have you ever noticed that you always do what you do and that you never do what you don't do? Amazing, isn't it?

As to your children, you might want to notice how I treat you since I am the father and mother and you are the son and daughter. I watch you and learn from you. Though I may occasionally experience infinite anxiety or wide-eyed disbelief as I watch you, I still trust you. If you treat your children the same way, they will live and grow. They will learn whatever you teach them, not by what you say but by who you are. Your children will either accept or reject who you are, but either way they will respond to who you are. And who you are will determine who they are. It can't be otherwise. The only way you work on or with your children is by what you do with yourself.

Me: I am again not sure what to do with what You are saying.

God: I repeat: do nothing.

Me: I can't do nothing.

God: I know.

Me: Then why would You ask me to do nothing?

God: I don't ask anything of you that you wouldn't ask of yourself. You ask the impossible of yourself every day, yet you are indignant when I ask the impossible of you.

Me: In what way do I ask the impossible of myself?

God: Each day you ask yourself to know what you do not know, to be where you are not and to have what you do not have. Each day you ignore your limitations while arguing for them. Each day you methodically forget who you are as you struggle to discover who you are. You spend each day occupied in hopes that things will work out sometime in the future. I ask you, are all of these not sufficiently impossible?

Me: Well, when You put it that way, they sound familiar, but not very much fun.

God: I didn't put it that way; you did. They ought to sound familiar, and I am delighted to hear you say that they don't sound like fun. Remember when I asked you if you were having fun? Your answer could have been, "Compared to what?" And my answer to that is, "Compared to infinite fun." You can have infinite fun while doing nothing. If there were a heaven, and there might be, it would be a place of infinite satisfaction with nothing to do and nowhere to get to. It would be one nation indivisible with liberty and justice for all. Do you know of such a place?

Me: I think so, but it doesn't look so much like heaven to me.

God: I know. But it could, you know.

Me: I don't see how.

God: Exactly.

Me: I do have a few ideas as to how You might be able to make my future a bit brighter.

God: I suspected that you did. Write a book. I am unwilling to hear one more set of wishes. You have what you need, actually much more than what you need, and I am mildly curious as to where you will go from here. You have my blessing and my love, but you do not yet have my sense of humor. A sense of humor might be a good place for you to start. One last hint: the moment you can find inspiration and humor in both the littlest and the biggest things you can think of, you will also find them in everything in between. When this happens, you won't be able to wipe the smile off your face, nor will you want to. I gave you paradise and I suggest that you might want to start recognizing it as such. Good luck. Have fun. And notice the obvious. We will talk again whenever we do.

2

My relationship with Emily took on new significance for me — whether I was tucking her into her crib, changing a diaper or watching her nurse in my wife's arms. My awareness and appreciation for God carried over to **all** parts of my life, so naturally, I hardly noticed it. The fact that I talked with God didn't make me special or important — lots of people talk to God. What was particularly interesting is that God spoke back to me and seemed to be interested in me. When I was a child I received some religious training but I never really considered myself to be religious. Frankly, I had very little to say on the subject of God because I wasn't even sure that I believed in God.

For some reason God had chosen to speak with me through Emily, and I was honored. It was in the evening that God spoke with me for the second time. Emily was five days old and asleep in my arms. I was gazing at Emily's perfect soft features when I heard God say…

God: Welcome.

Me: I was wondering if we would get another chance to speak. I am very pleased that we do. How are you tonight?

God: My condition does not vary, or, from your point of view, it varies so much that to answer your own question, all you have to do is look around you and see everything. Life and Earth are statements about how I am, not just some things, but all things.

Me: Will you tell me who is going to win the Super Bowl this year?

God: No. I have an infinite amount of time, no time, and still don't have enough time to watch sporting events. I have better things to do than to watch or even talk about sports. I did, however, get wind of a follow-up study with the winners of the national Little League baseball championship forty years after their big victory. The psychologists discovered that the big little winners referred to the championship an average of 2.5 times per day — forty years after the game was over! I am a bit curious that people can do just about anything, think anything or say anything, yet you often attempt to derive your importance from totally meaningless events and dwell on those events for years afterward. Haven't you got something better to think about?

Me: What would You suggest that we think about?

God: Another point of curiosity I have is just how lazy you can be. I am not suggesting anything; you figure out what is important and what is not; how you spend your time is up to you. I am just telling you that thus far, you are quite a boring species. It is possible that if you stop contriving things to be interested in you will discover what really interests you. You create what interests you out of nothing, not out of something. You are so busy doing something that you have forgotten who you are.

Me: But we have to stay busy. Our lives are so short that we must get everything done we can while we are alive.

God: You have to stay busy?

Me: Yes, we do. After all, doesn't what we do let us know who we are? I mean, I was a pretty good student and I have a good job. Surely that is important.

God: It is?

Me: Well, it must be; otherwise, why would I spend so much time working and doing things?

God: Exactly.

Me: There You go again. I don't understand what You mean. You seem to be saying that my job is not important. What is important? I like my job.

God: I am saying that your job is not important; nor is anyone's job — even mine. I don't really even have a job in the sense that you think of job. I am unemployed.

You know what is important. You persist in asking me things that you already know the answers to. You claim that you have a limited amount of time, so you must stay busy. You could just as easily say that you have a limited amount of time, so there is really nothing to do. You make the same statement, "I have limited time," and reach opposite conclusions from it. Pretty funny don't you think?

Me: The joke eludes me. You didn't make our lives long enough to really get a lot done. That is not so funny. Worse yet, we don't ever know when we are going to die.

God: Now you are getting to the really good jokes. I made your life just the right length to tempt you with how long it is and relieve you by its fleeting shortness. You don't dare do anything because then your life will seem endless, but you can't tackle anything too big because you might run out of time. I designed it this way to keep you from putting too much importance on what you do. It hasn't worked that way, though.

You are basically uncertain as to how long you will live, so the length of your life can't determine how you spend your time. The simplest thing in the world is uncertainty; it is certainty that is complicated. It takes variation to provide uncertainty, and it takes consistency to yield certainty. As a special present, just for your species, I have provided sufficient variation so that even I was not able to predict that you would try to squeeze certainty out of it. Low and behold, you hang on to certainty for dear life while missing the variation that would easily nurture you and allow you to loosen your grip. You are looking a gift horse in the mouth. I gave you uncertainty as a special gift, and you responded by acting as though the only thing you want is certainty. I did not give uncertainty to the deer, the mice or the foxes — and they don't hold to certainty. I gave you uncertainty and you have squandered it like it is meaningless. Go figure. I gave you uncertainty, so I suggest that you roll in it and rejoice in it at every turn. Uncertainty is a gift from God. Treat it as such.

Me: I don't quite understand what You mean.

God: Exactly so. You don't understand what I mean, this lack of understanding is your way of saying that you are not certain about it. I have just told you of the divine simplicity of uncertainty and given you some at the same time. And you ask me to explain myself so that you can become certain again. Certainty is one of your biggest liabilities, and I hope that is confusing to you.

Me: Can we move on?

God: I am rather enjoying myself. The one thing I don't get enough of is uncertainty, until I talk to you. If you could learn to derive pleasure from uncertainty to the same degree that you extract mock security from certainty, you would be constantly happy and pleased. You would have enough pleasure that you could pass it around freely. You could even become a prophet by pointing to the uncertainty that I filled Earth with. Uncertainty does not have to be made — it already exists.

You have built your culture a bit backwards by declaring that value is determined by scarcity. Gold and diamonds are valuable because they are rare. The fewer people who can have something, the more valuable it becomes. A baseball signed by Babe Ruth is more valuable after he dies because his death limits the supply. This is about as backward as it can be. Abundance is what determines value. The more abundant something is, the more valuable it must be. I gave you an abundance of anything worth having; to even consider it any other way is to blame me for your competition and shortages. I didn't give you very many diamonds because you don't need very many. **I gave you everything you need in the proportion that you need it.** I did not imagine that so many people would need diamond rings; I still can't. Use things in proportion to how I gave them to you, and put a premium on abundance — then your life will get easier. To do otherwise is to doubt God. Since uncertainty is the most constant and abundant thing you have, you could decide that it is the most valuable. There is enough uncertainty to go around; that is not an accident. Get a little uncertainty together, invite some friends and have a party.

Me: You have lost me now. It seems that so many religious leaders sell certainty for a price. Colleges sell certainty for a price, and our whole system is built on the obvious fact that the more certain I am, the better I am.

God: The fact that certainty is what your culture is built on does not make certainty a virtue. Your system has people attempt to get rid of what is most valuable and grab for what is most fleeting and worthless. When I created the world I did not add any certainty — granted, it was tempting to do so, but I resisted temptation. If I would have added certainty, then you would have been saddled with the whole right and wrong duality game. Some people could have been certain of the right things while others would have been certain of the wrong things. No, certainty would have been a terrible thing to put on Earth. It is not easy to amaze God, but you do it often by the way you create certainty and then claim that you have found it. **Certainty does not exist; it is always an illusion.**

As for paying money to get certainty, money isn't really of value and neither is certainty. I should think that you wouldn't want to reward someone for coming up with something as ridiculous as certainty, so you might not want to buy any more of it. An economy based on certainty or scarcity is bankrupt. A species that is certain will compete and fight for the right illusion.

Me: Are You saying that money doesn't have any value?

God: Yes, that is not only what I am saying, but it is also what is true; I don't know how to lie. It seems that sometimes you forget who you are talking to.

Me: Well, if money is not of value, then can I borrow some? What the heck, You're God, can I borrow a lot?

God: I don't have any.

Me: None at all?

God: None at all. But, if you want money so badly, I can arrange it so that you win the lottery.

Me: You could do that?

God: Of course.

Me: Will You?

God: Sure. I usually don't bother with such things, but in hopes of teaching you something, I will have you win the lottery next month. You won't like it, though. After the excitement wears off, you will discover that you are no different regardless of how much of that printed paper you have. You will have the same problems. If you are like most lottery winners, who had little money before they won the lottery, you will probably end up with no more money than you started with. If you really want something of value, I could give you the ability to see uncertainty and delight in it.

Me: You persist with this talk about uncertainty. I am certain that I would be happy if I won the lottery.

God: Exactly. Certainty always comes right before a fall. That is one of those things that you miss over and over again. You can win the lottery if you want too, but it won't do anything for you.

Me: Come to think of it, I really do want to win the lottery, and if I win it, then I won't want to win it anymore. So winning the lottery would be comparable to selling my want.

God: Now you're talking. It just might be that humans make the mistake of thinking that wanting things is unsatisfying and having things is satisfying. It is just the other way around. **Wanting things is endless, while having things is terminal.** Let's leave it with you wanting to win the lottery: you will find someday that wanting is a more vital part of you than having. If you learn the difference in pleasure between wanting and having soon enough, you may not have to completely destroy your planet manufacturing things to have.

Me: Thanks for this conversation. It has been very enlightening and useful.

God: It has?

Me: Yes, I have a lot to think about.

God: You do? People never cease to amaze me.

Me: I am glad You find us so entertaining.

God: Me, too. Until next time, I wish you uncertainty and pleasure. One parting word about how long you will live: very few people leave the Earth without their quota of certainty. I cannot say more about the fill of certainty you personally require before you leave, but I can tell you that the more uncertain you are while on Earth, the longer you will be there. What happens after you leave Earth is another thing — a thing that it would be very healthy for you to be uncertain about. Goodbye.

3

After my initial conversations with God, I found myself spending more time with Emily and Judson. Sometimes we would play games, but usually we would just curl up together and tell stories. I invented tales about imaginary people and places and events that ranged from heroic to hilarious. We also talked about the universe, life and other things that I thought were real. I talked to Emily, a baby, as if she understood just what I said. I discovered later that she understood **everything**.

Although I spent hours thinking about my conversations with God, I am embarrassed to admit that it took me two months to initiate a conversation with God. I waited passively for God to speak. Then, one night as I watched Emily sleeping, I spoke to God and to my surprise God spoke back.

Me: God, I have been waiting for our next meeting and I think it is time. I have some big questions.

God: Go Ahead.

Me: Oh! Okay. When do I get to be You?

God: Are you sure you want to be me?

Me: From our talks so far, I have gleaned a number of things, one of which is that the more I am like You, the better I am. So it makes sense that if I work at it hard enough, someday I get to be You.

God: It doesn't make sense to me. I am not sure that the universe is ready for two of me. There have been many ancient societies based on multiple Gods, and most of them are long gone. If I am the God of everything, then what would you be the God of? Would I have to give up some of what I am God of so that you could be God of that?

Me: I am not sure exactly how it would work. I should think that we could just let the details work themselves out. Did You have to plan things to become God in the first place?

God: I didn't plan on being God. I have never been anything else. About the details sorting themselves out — I am not so sure about that. Perhaps it would be useful for you to look around your Earth to the people who think that they are the most like God or even think that they are God.

Me: From what I have heard, there are many people who think that they are God, but most of them are in institutions. There are also some people who say that they have a direct line to You, such as religious leaders or politicians. Then there are the new-agers who say that they are God or that who they are is God.

God: Which of these three groups is having the most fun?

Me: Well, I'm not sure. It seems that the new-agers are not particularly happy. They just keep incorporating the fad of the moment into their language. Although the reasons for their behaviors and dysfunctions are insightful, I'm not sure whether their insights ever influence their behaviors. They seem to talk more about being God than actually behaving Godlike. The new-agers' approach seems too meaning-full to be fun. The preachers and politicians don't seem to have much fun because they are constantly trying to stay ahead of the evidence that they are not God or even Godlike. They seem so intent on avoiding scandal; it would be easy to come to the conclusion that they all have something to hide. Both politicians and religious leaders are too serious to be having much fun. That just leaves the people in institutions who say they are God. I don't know much about them because they are in the institutions; I guess they are there so that I don't have any contact with them.

God: Do you begin to get the idea that you are not supposed to be God? I never suggested that you be God. I did suggest that it would benefit you greatly if you would act more like I do, which means, generally, to be inactive. You have a job, which is being a person, and I suggest you get good at it. You are a person, aren't you?

Me: Yes.

God: Then I guess it would make sense for you to explore what it is to be a person. I once saw a man teaching pigs to fly. Even though he became absorbed in teaching them, he was not successful. No part of being a pig has to do with flying. The man who was attempting to teach the pigs never ran short of pork, nor did he have any flying pigs. Every species on Earth has its areas of expertise and its drawbacks. One of the rules of Earth is that you remain the species that you are — it is a waste of time to attempt to be some other species, and it can even be dangerous. A butterfly attempting to be a frog is at best a waste of time. But this is a silly example since the only species that attempts to be something it is not is humans. Whether you know it or not, most people already think they are God. They think the universe revolves around them, which, by the way, is a simple definition of God. These same people don't even know that they think they are God. **But again, with the littlest bit of examination, it will become obvious that to be as self-centered as most people are, considering how fallible they are, requires some sort of personal deification.**

I suggest that it would be most beneficial for you to assume that you are not God and that you are a person. If you really are God, this assumption won't hurt you, and if you are not God, it could save you a great deal of suffering. You are not meant to be God: you are meant to be a person. That is exactly why you look the way you do.

Me: I was wondering about that. What do You look like?

God: If I let you see me once, you would be doomed to attempt to look like me for the rest of your life, an effort that would never be worth the struggle. If I appeared to a few people and they discovered that my hair is parted in the middle, there would soon be whole groups of people parting their hair in the middle and declaring war on anyone who did not.

Me: Do You part your hair in the middle?

God: You see what I mean? No, I don't part my hair in the middle, I don't part it at all and I part it at every point and at only the exact point at which it should be parted. You should see my hair: it is beautiful and I don't have any.

Me: Now You are making fun of me. Are You really bald?

God: Well, yes and no.

Me: Which is it?

God: The less you know about my appearance, the better off you will be. Work on your own appearance. When I speak of appearance, I am not speaking of cosmetic or superficial looks — I mean the way you appear. In this context, appearance and existence are synonymous. If I let you know that I had attended Yale, you would use that information to create a problem for Harvard. The less you know about me, the better; and the more you discover about yourself, the better. I am not speaking to you to have you learn about me; **I am speaking to you to have you learn about you.** I provide you with a completely noncommittal entity — Me — outside of yourself. You can adopt my lack of commitment in the pursuit of who you are. You can then look at yourself impartially and with greater love and compassion than you have heretofore imagined. This perspective would allow you to move out of the middle ground, where people spend their whole lives, and embrace extremes, seemingly opposing extremes, at the same time.

Me: Once again You have lost me. Are You saying that I, as a human being, am a species of compromise and that I shouldn't be?

God: Yes, I am saying that and much more. Not only have you staked out the middle ground, but there is no middle ground. You have compromised yourself so thoroughly that there is nothing left. This particular nothing goes up for sale in the marketplace daily. You have built a mock economy, a mock psychology, a mock philosophy and a mock world. You have argued so strongly for the middle ground that you have nothing left. You must return to extremes, all extremes: that is where life occurs. You cannot return to one extreme without its opposite; attempting to do so has gotten you into trouble. You must embrace opposites, which will lead you farther from the center in both directions at the same time. You will not stretch, but the center ground you cling to so thoroughly will disappear. In this process you will lose nothing but illusion since the middle ground never did exist.

As it is, people are on thin ice, habitually following the leader and moving slowly or stopping altogether to avoid any risk. The way to walk on thin ice is to keep moving and to walk as lightly as you can. Never put your weight in any one place for long. The wind treats ice quite well, influencing it deeply, but never falling through. The wind can blow a piece of ice for hundreds of miles but never get wet. You might want to adopt some of the lightness of the wind and abandon your caution.

Me: I don't understand. It is good to compromise; certainly it is good to reach understanding and a point of common communication with other people. Surely you can't be saying that we should turn our backs on each other.

God: I am not saying that you **should** — I am saying that you **have** without even knowing it. Other people have become your second biggest problem, surpassed only by the problems you cause for yourself. I am suggesting that people are not really separate and that the very compromises you call communication and commerce make you appear to be separate. Society is a formalization of rules made up to keep people in line on a non-existent playing field: an unnatural line where there need not be a barrier at all. Walking this line makes you predictable. Predictability is anti-evolutionary. Have you ever noticed that most people are not satisfied? Many of them have even given up the possibility of being satisfied. What most people call satisfaction is so hollow and thin that it could not sustain a flea, let alone a person. You folks are wasting away, starving yourselves to death without even knowing it. As a species you are becoming desperate, but you are so busy that you don't even notice it. Humor and pleasure, in the most simple things or nothing at all, have disappeared as you call your present state of desperation "progress." Some people notice it, but if they point it out, they are either ignored or misinterpreted. I am reminded of that great story of the *Emperor's New Clothes*. I went around naked for weeks after reading it. Human beings are so strange. The same species that can produce a Beethoven symphony can trade money for health (health for money) and leave a baby for a job. You can discover the intricacies of time through music and miss the most obvious rules and basis of your very existence. You can starve to death where food is abundant.

Me: You are saying so much, but it seems a bit like I am being bawled out by an angry parent. Can't You be a little easier on us? We are doing our best. While I still leave my children for my job, I have noticed that during the past two months I have spent much more time with my children. And, I'm thinking of leaving my job so I can spend all of my time with my family. I know I would be healthier, but it doesn't seem fiscally responsible.

God: I apologize. Sometimes I get a little carried away. I talk to each species in its own native tongue, but try as I might, effective communication through human speech remains out of my grasp. Sometimes I attempt to make up for the ineffectiveness of human communication with my vehemence. All I mean to say is that the human race is in trouble, and part of the problem is that you don't even know it. I want you to know it, and I sometimes forget that telling you is not sufficient. Not only are you in trouble, but doing more of what got you in trouble will not get you out.

Me: I know we are in trouble. My question for You is, what shall we do about it?

God: There you go again, asking for help that you don't need. I am not your employee, you know. You want to tell me what to do; you want me to work for you. I don't work. I won't work. You can easily discover what to do. It is obvious. If I tell you what to do, you will be dependent on me — I won't have that. You must begin to notice and appreciate the simple and obvious rather than always moving to the more complex.

Me: Are you saying that life is simple?

God: No, I am not saying that **life** is simple. I am saying that **living** is simple, at least as simple as dying. Living is easy while you are alive. Sometimes, as I look around

Earth, I have a difficult time determining which objects are animate and which ones are inanimate. I used to think that the inanimate objects were more predictable than the animate ones, but some humans are becoming so predictable that they look virtually inanimate. I do not suggest that you work to become inanimate. That is something you were never meant to be. The more animate you are, the more life flows through you. Your illusion of time is not as fixed as you think. Spending your time being animated influences the illusion more than an inanimate existence. Your life is as long as you have it be. It is the degree of animation you muster which determines not the **length of time**, but the **amount of life** that you have.

Me: What do you mean by animated? It seems contradictory to tell us not to do anything and also to be animated.

God: It is indeed contradictory, from your point of view. Animation has something to do with potential activity and awareness of possibilities, not with the doing of anything or nothing. The more you can take in and perceive, the more animated you are. The more you can let flow through you without holding onto anything, the more animated you will be. Predictability requires repetition and damming the flow. A rock in a stream wears down slowly with little appreciation for the process of its disappearance or ultimate merging with the stream. The rock is ever changing, but the changes are so small at each moment that it is hard to perceive them.

The rock has one way to relate to the water — it must resist the water, giving up as little of itself as it can to maintain its rock-like form as long as possible. You as a person have many more alternatives than the rock. These alternatives and your realization of them (not the acting out of them) are the source of your animation.

Me: Would You then say it is always best to have more alternatives than fewer alternatives?

God: Yes, for your species to have the most life possible, alternatives are necessary, and the more the merrier. The middle ground of compromise is an exhaustion of alternatives: it may be a level playing field, but the level is low. Do you understand the point of adopting opposing extremes in this light?

Me: I think I do, but it certainly doesn't sound very easy. Then again, I guess what people are doing now isn't easy either. I will work a bit with the exploration of opposites, though the whole idea of it is a bit upsetting to me. I will also stop attempting to be God and will begin to discover any Godlike behaviors in myself.

I have one last question. How do I know when I am on the right track?

God: You are on the right track when you find yourself being pleased for no reason at all — when you find yourself enjoying life more each day without even knowing why. I designed Earth as a place for you to be born —

able to learn, explore and play for a lifetime, and then leave. I never intended that things should become so serious and important. Earth is made for all species to play on and for no species to dominate or to get an inordinate amount of anything. Human beings are presently hoarding suffering, and that has to stop so that the balance can return on Earth. I never imagined that a species would hamster away suffering as the human race does. I suggest that you give up your collections of suffering and problems and return to the kind of play that many of your children rejoice in until they learn better (or worse). Until our next conversation, have fun and play more than you ever have before. I won't be watching you, but it will be obvious on our next visit if you have been playing. Good-bye.

Me: Good-bye, God, and thanks for the conversation.

4

fter I discovered that I could start the conversations, God seemed much more interested in
talking to me. Our next conversation took
place two days later while Emily and I were playing
together on the living room rug. This little piggy had
gone to market so many times that I had lost interest
and was thinking about business. While my body was
present, my mind was far away. Just as I noticed that
Emily had fallen asleep, God spoke.

God: Where would you like to start today?

Me: I have a few problems and I need Your help. I have
a big business proposal to present next week, and I
am very nervous about it. Can You help me with it?

God: What sort of help would you like?

Me: Well, I guess I would like to know how it will turn
out. Will the client accept my proposal? Will I get that

raise I have been after? And how will my kids turn out? When will I know if I am a good parent?

God: The moment you pretend that you have a future, the flood gates open and the problems rush through.

Me: What do You mean, **pretend**? I do have a future.

God: You do?

Me: Don't I? I mean, I must have a future since I spend so much time preparing for it. This week I would like to have spent more time with my wife and kids, but I had to get this proposal ready. If there were no future, I would live my life very differently.

God: I have bad news for you...you have no future. There is no such thing as the future, and all of your planning is in vain.

Me: You're kidding, right?

God: Nope.

Me: But there must be a future. Things are going to get better soon, and when they get better, I'll be satisfied. Please tell me there is a future, or I guess this will be one case in which You will have Your opinion and I will have mine. Without a future there would be no hope at all.

God: Exactly. The existence of the future is not a matter of opinion. There is no future, never has been and never will be. Get it?...Never will be — it's a joke.

Me: You take away my future and make jokes about it!? That is a little like laughing at a funeral. You wouldn't laugh at a funeral, would You?

God: I wouldn't go to a funeral, partially for fear of laughing. You people take yourselves so seriously. Just because death looks like an end to you, that doesn't make it an end. Death could just as easily be a beginning. You have a sacred cow called the future. A sacred bull is more like it. You depend on the future for what you are unwilling to have in the present. What would life be like if you acted as if you had no future? What would be the repercussions of such a radical and accurate approach?

Me: It seems I would miss out on everything. Life would not be worth living. I could not go on.

God: You're being a little melodramatic, don't you think? Without the future you would have to either be in the past or the present. There is no past, so let's just pick the present for your setting.

Me: You can't do away with the past that quickly.

God: Oh, yes I can. It takes no time at all to have no time. There is no past and no future, and living under such imaginary constraints opens the door for ignoring **what is** and worrying about what **will be** and **what was**. The idea of time is an interesting one, but it is just a theory developed to force order on things. You invented the future and the past, and then immediately the problem of not having enough time arose. You discovered that when you are suffering, time goes more slowly, so you started suffering more just to get more time. Have you ever noticed that when you are having fun, time passes quickly, and that when you are having an awful time, when you are in pain or when you are suffering, time passes slowly?

Me: Well, yes, I have noticed that. When I have a cold or fever, time seems to stand still. Even if I have something like my proposal to worry about, time seems to go more slowly.

God: That's it. Worry, pain, suffering and problems are just symptoms of living with your illusion called time. Pretending that there is a past and a future confines you to learning from the past and preparing for the future. The present gets neglected and is only attended to when new problems or intense experiences occur. By making a problem big enough, close enough, painful enough, long enough or often enough, you are forced to notice the present and attend to the problem. If you do away with the illusion of past and future, you could bypass the whole **have-a-problem-get-attention syndrome** since the present would receive all of your attention every moment.

Me: Is it really that simple?

God: Yes.

Me: Let's get practical for a moment. Theory is fine, but I need to know how the presentation will go so that I can stop worrying about it.

God: Have you been listening? There is no presentation. Being practical has to do with the present and nothing to do with the illusions you call the future and the past. I have noticed that when the going gets tough, people depend on the future for hope or the past for consolation. Nowhere is this more obvious than in a relationship. A person falls in love with someone and temporarily loses himself or herself in the delight of their moments together. This person accumulates enough of these great moments to justify getting married and promising to spend more time together. The more time they spend together, the less wild they are for each other. They begin taking each other for granted. They recall the great times, hope that wonderful times are lurking in the future and ignore the present.

The whole idea of time allows you to lose interest and tests your attention span, another novel human invention. You were not born with an attention span. I did not give you one because I did not give you time. Without time, all you have is attention — a span requires a beginning and an end. Get it?

Me: You seem to be saying that all we have is the present, but that would mean that we would have to live each moment as though it matters. We would live each moment as if it might be our last. We would never procrastinate, and we would do exactly what we wanted at each moment.

God: Would that be so bad? Part of your difficulty in understanding the illusion of time is that you have always been taught the common sense fact that you cannot always do what you want. You must delay gratification and must often do what you are told. You must bow to the little mock gods around you and do what you are supposed to do. Just to make your condition a little more stable, society tells you that doing what you want to do all the time is selfish, and you wouldn't want to be selfish, would you? While this approach may serve to make people more predictable, it results again in suffering and oppression. It amuses me to think of the power that you people have, going to such extensive illusionary ends to make things worse than they are.

Me: But what about my proposal?

God: What about your proposal?

Me: How will it turn out?

God: The way it does.

Me: That is clear enough and obvious, but it doesn't do me any good.

God: Now we are getting somewhere, though there is nowhere to get to. Yes, it is obvious that your proposal will go the way it does — remember that "obvious" is what you want to learn to attend to. It does not do you any good to know that your presentation will go the way it does, but it doesn't do you any bad either. Are you willing to open the door on good and let bad in at the same time?

Me: Well, I would rather have the good without the bad.

God: That can't be done, even by God. If you get the good, you get the bad in equal measure. But you just lied to me. You said that you would like to have the good without the bad. If that were the case, you would win much more often. It is the threat of failure that gets you moving much faster than the carrot of success. Your whole culture, with few exceptions, is dependent on failure or at least the fear of failure. I could fix it so that your proposal goes very well, but you would end up hating me if I did so and you knew about it. If there were not the possibility for failure, you could not take any credit for success. How many times would you watch a football game if you knew the outcome? It is the uncertainty of the outcome that keeps your attention. I could have you always know what is going to happen before it does. As a matter of fact, you already have that ability, but you don't use it because everything you presently call fun in your life would be lost. You would lose the uncertainty that you thrive on, feed on and attempt to diminish.

Me: Are you saying that I don't want to know the future?

God: I am saying that you already **can** know the future (remember that future and past are both illusions) and that the fact that you ignore this ability makes it more than obvious that you don't want to know the future or that you love wanting to know the future while believing that you can't know it. You use the certainty (**mock certainty**) of the past and the uncertainty (**mock uncertainty**) of the future to keep yourself suspended in the illusion of time while calling the whole process life. I call it a magic act, "Look, Ma, no strings": a whole species floating in mid-air with no strings attached. You are very amusing, and I appreciate it and love you for it. I just wish you could share in the joke with me. You use the illusion of time to add uncertainty when, in fact, there is infinite uncertainty around already without your adding the illusion of uncertainty. You may find the illusion of uncertainty easier to deal with than uncertainty itself, but they are not the same thing. Real uncertainty nourishes you while illusionary uncertainty starves you.

Me: So I could know how my proposal is going to go? Is that what you are saying?

God: No, I am not saying that you **could**; I am saying that you **do**. You know beyond a shadow of a doubt, and you won't let yourself know that you know because you would rob yourself of the delicious anguish of uncertainty and potential failure that makes your life longer by having the time before your presentation pass more slowly. It's a neat system you have. It is obvious to every species who cares to look at it. And, like water to the fish and air to the bird, this obvious state of the human species is least obvious to yourselves.

Let's try a little experiment. (God holds out two imaginary hands.) Pick a hand. (The person chooses a hand, and in it is a large diamond.)

Me: Wow, is this real?

God: As real as it can be. (God holds out two hands again.) Pick one.

Me: Another diamond! You may not make me happy, but you are going to make me rich.

(This process is repeated numerous times. The number of times the person is willing to play the game relates directly to the size of the diamond. The larger the diamond, the longer someone will play.)

God: Pick a hand.

Me: Wait a minute. Either you have a diamond in each hand or I am a very good guesser because I win the diamond every time.

God: I will not wait; that is a human phenomenon. How do you know that winning is getting the diamond? That might be losing.

Me: It couldn't be. Now tell me, do you have a diamond in each hand or am I just a good guesser?

God: I'll never tell. Remember, it was you who always wanted to win. If I have a diamond in each hand, then you always get to win. That game you would certainly enjoy and want to play forever.

Me: In spite of all the diamonds, I must admit that I don't want to play anymore if You have a diamond in each hand. I have to agree with You that it is not even a game unless one hand does not have a diamond. If one hand does not have one, and the other does, then it is by my talent that I earn the diamond. I guess it is the possibility of both failure and success that makes a game a game. And I do love games.

God: Yes, you do love games, and it is precisely the opportunity for success and failure that motivates you. Very few humans want to play if they know they will always win. I won't fix it so that your proposal goes well; that would rob you of both the game and the satisfaction of a job well done. Sadly, many humans have learned to play the pick-a-hand diamond game without a diamond in either hand — **a guaranteed loss is interpreted as reinforcement of pessimism and thus is rewarding in and of itself.** It doesn't look like much fun, but still there are a lot of people playing that game. After a while, they couldn't even see a diamond if it was there. Knowing the future would remove the source of motivation for you, at least in the illusion you call life.

Me: You're right. I don't really want to know how the proposal will turn out. To state it more accurately, I do want to know, but I enjoy the wanting and the game of not knowing.

God: Congratulations. Now I have a question for you. Will you explain this process of earning something, deserving something or not appreciating something unless you have suffered, slaved or worked to get it? I don't understand this and don't even know where it came from. It is not something that I put in when I created Earth. You are the only species I see with it. If a wolf has an easy kill, he appreciates the easy meal, but if you have an easy sale, you celebrate it much less than if it had been a hard one. The longer and harder you work for something, the more important you say it is. You say such things as "No pain no gain" or "Nothing great is possible without great effort." Could you please explain this to me?

Me: I don't know that I can. It is just the way things are. I have noticed this tendency in myself, and it seems to work for me.

God: I was hoping you could explain it better than that. It is not natural. It leads to a lot of hard work and a loss of a sense of humor. Never before have I seen a species who will take the long way around just because there is virtue and struggle in it. When I designed you, I made everything easy. If you ever perceive anything as difficult, the difficulty is something you added. I designed Earth to be an easy, fun place, and it amuses me that many of your oppressive illusions have come about in my name.

Me: Are you saying we don't need to work as hard as we do?

God: Bingo. You don't have to work at all. Your work is doubly hard because you not only need to do the work, but you then have to believe it means something about your worth. It is impossible to create worth. Self worth is something you discover. The evidence is all around you, **always**. You could rename the forty-hour work week an every moment discovery week and you would not only have more fun, but you would also get more done.

Me: Are you saying that I should quit my job?

God: No, I am only saying what I am saying, and your job is neither important enough to quit or to keep. Centuries ago (if we pretend that there is a past) people were hunters and gatherers. They gathered and hunted for two or three hours a day, nourished themselves and played for the rest of each day. Now you extend your work week by putting in overtime and then needing unwind-time with such distractions as drugs, drinks, TV and other contrived entertainment. When do you enjoy life? I vividly remember a tribe of people in England called The Balancers, who hunted and gathered as little as possible and spent the rest of their waking hours learning to balance things on different parts of their bodies. It is truly amazing what they balanced and where. I am impressed with what they learned both about themselves and about Earth through their balancing.

Me: I have never heard of such a tribe.

God: You may not have heard of them directly, but it is through their marvelous play that you have a system of weights and measures. Everything that you are doing now arose out of play and humor. You have become too effective at removing the play and humor and adding seriousness. I suspect that you would not have a high opinion of a person who ate the peel of the banana and discarded the tasty middle part. That is, in effect, what you are doing as you miss the ease and fun of life while hoarding the suffering.

Me: Is everything really easy?

God: Easier. Now, until next time, there is no next time. If you have learned anything from this talk, things might be a little easier for you. At the very least, you ought to derive a little entertainment from the pain, effort and struggle that you put yourself through. Don't laugh too often. It isn't possible. Good-bye.

5

Emily was three months old, and I couldn't remember what life was like without her. It had been two weeks since my last chat with God and it had been no time at all. Living beyond my model of time had made it much easier to be present in the moment. With the Holidays around the corner, I'd noticed that my seasonal nostalgia and grumpiness had slipped away, making room for joy and humor. I still thought about work when I was at home, and my thoughts ventured homeward while at work, but I caught myself in the process. There was just too much evidence for the existence of time for me to throw it out, at least **now**.

My wife and I replaced Emily's bedroom nightlight with a string of Christmas lights. After the house was quiet, I went into her room and began talking with God.

Me: I am surprised. Since we began our little chats, I am much happier. I find myself smiling and laughing independent of my circumstances. I am beginning to think You are right about how easy life can be.

God: Congratulations.

Me: Congratulations are hardly in order since it doesn't seem as if I have **done** anything to be happier. My pleasure, in the simplest things, is just coming about on its own. I don't know what causes it.

God: There you go again wanting to work hard or not take credit when effort was not expended. About causes: **causes are not for you to know.** I did not equip you to know about causes. You can see effects, but causes are a bit beyond your small frame of reference.

Me: But I do know what causes some things; I just don't know what caused my increase in pleasure.

God: Your interpretation of a cause just indicates where you have stopped in the process of figuring something out. It is like a bus station: never a destination, always just a temporary stop-over. Have you ever noticed that nobody goes to a bus station just to go to that bus station? They are always on the way to somewhere else or there to do a job. **Your interpretations of cause are just an indication of a little break in your transition from one perspective to another.**

Me: You keep threatening what I think is firm ground. What can I know for sure? Please give me one thing I can be sure of.

God: You can be sure of anything.

Me: You're right about that, but what should I be sure of?

God: It doesn't matter. You seem to be asking me what would be the right thing to be sure of. That question is entirely dependent on where you are and what you are aware of at the moment. One thing I strongly recommend is that you change what you are sure of quite often because otherwise your tendency is toward such consistency that you become almost inanimate. So, if you want to be sure of the one right certainty, have it be your changeability.

Me: Your answers have a way of leaving me more confused than I was before I asked my question. Yet even through my confusion, I can tell that You are answering a question somewhat bigger than the one I ask. I like that, even though it is a bit unsettling.

God: What shall we discuss?

Me: Something has been bothering me. Why did You invent death?

God: I didn't.

Me: Just when I was beginning to like You and even trust You, there goes Your credibility again. What do You mean, You didn't create death?

God: I didn't create death. You created death. You invented death because the idea of eternity was a little too daunting for you. You also created death to lend a little more credibility to your thoughts and opinions.

The threat of death — a constant threat to many people — is an excuse to attempt to make what you do important. You seem to continually need something to worry about, and death is a big worry on Earth. Disease is another of your inventions that I think you would have been better without.

Me: One thing I am sure of is that I did not invent death. I would like to live forever.

God: Are you sure you did not invent death?

Me: Yes.

God: Did you invent life?

Me: No, You did.

God: Yes, I did invent life, but so do you, every moment. I invented life, but I did not invent death. There is no such thing as death. The whole idea of death, that there could be a cease in the flow and process of the universe, is a bit funny. From your perspective, your tiny location, life seems to end. It doesn't cease at all. If you have a problem with one perspective, all you have to do is change your perspective. Certainly, in your life, you will have changes in perspective — little ones and big ones. When a change in perspective is big enough, you call it death, which does not make it death. It just means that you call it death. One of your esteemed presidents, Abraham Lincoln, once asked, "How many legs does a dog have if you call its tail a leg?" His answer was four, because calling a tail a leg doesn't make it a leg.

When you are holding tightly to an illusion, the loss of any part of that illusion looks a bit like death. What you call death is a radical shift in perspective. When you go to a movie, the movie appears to end. If you liked the movie, you might wish it had gone on, but you can always see it again or hold out for the sequel. If you didn't care for the movie, you act relieved that it is over. Your approach to radical shifts in perspective is much the same. If you are really enjoying this particular perspective you call life, you wish it would go on forever and never change, though it always changes anyway. If you are not enjoying your current perspective, you bring life to a standstill and wish life would change, maybe. Strangely enough, you use death as an excuse to live a shallow and worthless existence so that you won't have much to lose when the radical change in perspective comes. From my perspective, you never lose anything, and the process goes on. There is no such thing as death. There are not really any things at all. Death is a shift in perspective — that is all. Death is the movement from one illusion to another. If you think you are the illusion, then death looks like an end.

Me: I am not sure I follow You, but I am quite sure You are mistaken about death.

God: I do not mean that you personally created death. You subscribe to the habit of death much as you might subscribe to some periodical. So many people have had the radical shift you call death that you are certain you will, too; in other words, you bought the farm. You can cancel your subscription to the habit of death.

Me: How would I go about doing that?

God: I, God, declare that from this moment on, you are immortal.

Me: That is all there is to it? I am afraid that I don't, I can't, believe You.

God: Whether you believe me or not makes no difference to your immortality. I am not suggesting that your exact perspective will exist forever. But, of course, since there is no such thing as time, it will. It might be easier for you to understand this as a process. Things change. You change. Sometimes you notice the change; sometimes you don't. Sometimes the change is small and sometimes it is big. Sometimes the change is so **small** that you don't notice it and often it is so **big** that you don't notice it. What you call death is a change so large that you don't notice it. You miss so much, but missing a radical shift as large as death is scary to you. Pay attention — that way you can enjoy and learn from all radical shifts, large and small, including death.

I am including a lot of inaccuracy in my explanation, and I apologize for it. I am doing so in an attempt to be understood. I am attempting to pretend that change and time exist so that you will understand a little more about the **impossibility of death**. You couldn't have death if you wanted to. Suicide is one of the least significant acts available to you. One of the most significant is living. **Living is too important to take seriously.**

Me: You are telling me that I am immortal?

God: Yes and no.

Me: There You go again.

God: Sorry, it all depends on what you mean by the "I" in your question. The smaller you can make the "I" in your question, the more terminal death appears to be. The bigger the "I" is, the more obvious is your immortality. I did not make life something that needs to be hoarded or stowed away in a closet for a rainy day. I made life something to use and pass around. Even your so-called different species are not as different as you may think. You share life with all other species and everything on Earth. You and Earth, are one nation indivisible under me. As long as anything is existent, everything is existent. Arguments for your perspective make the "I" small and rob you of the perspective of the process around you. Process does not end, and it does not get interrupted.

Me: So You are saying that if I am big enough, then I am immortal? That must be why there are so many fat people around—they are striving to become big enough to be immortal.

God: There you go joking about death. Remember when I mentioned laughing at a funeral and you took offense?

Me: Yes, that seems long ago.

God: No time, believe me. Laughing at a funeral or, better yet, celebrating is very appropriate. Radical shifts, small shifts, or no shifts at all: the more of these you can celebrate, the more you get to celebrate.

Me: This all seems too simple and obvious when I am talking to You. I hope I remember it after our chat. The bigger my perspective of who "I" am, the easier it is for me to perceive my immortality. Immortality is not something I have to learn or earn; it is mine, whether I like it or not.

God: You've got it. It only matters to **you** whether or not you perceive your immortality; it doesn't matter to your immortality at all. Conversely, it only matters to you that you perceive that you are immortal, not that you are really immortal. You often think that appearance is everything, though it is so little.

Me: How do I go about having a bigger perspective of who "I" am?

God: That is simple to tell you, but impossible for people to do — it doesn't take doing. The more perspectives and the more different the perspectives you maintain at the same time, the bigger you become. Flexibility of thought and tolerance of paradox (in fact, appreciation for paradox and opposites) are all important. With flexibility, you leave your judgments behind and become entirely accepting. The less you resist, the bigger you become and the more you are like the flow of the stream rather than the rock in the stream. You flow on as a part of the stream and are not worn down or battered by it. The same stream that wears down a rock is a playground for fish. I suggest that the way to increase the size of your perspective is to **vary both your location and what you perceive your location to be**.

At the same time that you play with having the "I" be bigger, I suggest that you work on making yourself smaller. Bigger includes smaller; it is smaller that does not include bigger.

Me: I think I understand what You are saying, but I am not quite sure yet how to go about it.

God: That's easy, as is everything. If you think you know something, change what you know. Develop the ability to be certain of two opposite things at the same time. Adopt all opinions on an issue. Have what you think become a source of entertainment rather than a place to stand. **The firmer your footing, the smaller your perspective.** Loosen your footing and look around. You will be amazed and entertained by the pleasure you can have when you are not holding on to anything tightly. If you fell from a cliff and grabbed onto a small branch growing part way down, the rocks below would look like a threat to your life from such a position rather than looking like a source of enjoyment. In such a situation, you might miss the delightful cloud patterns overhead and the intricate texture and shape of the tree that is apparently saving your life.

Your illusions put you in just such a position, not really, but in your perspective, which is all you have. You are balanced precariously above your death, hoping that you don't fall. You are holding on for dear life and wondering why life is not too much fun. You are not at risk; you are not in jeopardy of death or even problems in life. As you learn to embrace your immortality, everything will get easier, especially the things you have feared.

You can do no wrong, or right either. You are not precarious at all and, ironically, the tree limbs that you hold to so tightly are just your illusions. Swinging on illusions places you in jeopardy because at any moment they can be shown to be the illusions they are. Holding to your thoughts and opinions, you have chosen the least stable thing you can find to save you from both life and death. **From your perspective, death looks real and life is theoretical; in fact, life is real and death is theoretical.** As life becomes easier, it will become obvious that death has always been impossible for you. You can let go, and as you do, you will appreciate more of yourself and all that is around you as **you** include more.

Me: I think I am beginning to understand. I like this immortality stuff. But earlier You mentioned that You did not invent sickness. What did You mean by that?

God: Sickness is a habit and a perspective shift somewhat less radical than death. It is of the same kind, but not as extreme. Like death, it is an illusion. Sickness is a means to get attention and to make life sufficiently uncomfortable so that it seems longer.

All disease is habit of thought perpetrated on the body. I find particularly interesting the turns your society takes. Sometimes it is the most well-meaning person who falls into the most obvious holes. There are people on Earth discovering that they can work to heal their bodies with their minds, and they seem so excited about misusing their minds in this way. It is thinking that has produced the habits labeled disease. This approach of using the mind to heal the body is a bit like putting the fox in charge of the hen house or the hypochondriac in charge of the medicine cabinet. Your thinking is the problem. Without your thinking, there would be no disease or problems. You don't have the option not to think, but you can take your thinking more or less seriously. **Disease happens when you take your thinking seriously, and entertainment is the result of taking your thoughts lightly.**

The more amused you become, the healthier you will be. When you reveal the illusionary nature of an illusion, the consequences of that illusion become humorous. If you were threatened by something invisible that did not even exist, it wouldn't be much of a threat, would it?

You can literally make yourself sick, but it is difficult to make yourself well; it is much easier to just stop making yourself sick. Lighten up, discover the **humor** and the life in and around you, and you will not get sick often, and when you do, it will be no more important than a trivial historical novel. Sickness as a habit is no more important than a tragic novel.

Me: It sounds as though you are saying that I not only don't have to die, I also don't have to get sick. Dying and sickness are all a matter of how I live. How I live makes health, sickness, life and death possible.

God: It is how you live that makes death and disease possible, so it is obviously how you live that makes life and health possible as well. Are you having fun yet?

Me: More so all the time. This conversation has lightened my load. I even **feel** lighter.

God: That sounds like progress to me. It is time for you to go out and play again. You have been in a dilemma. **You are a little like a camel in that you are a beast of burden who complains bitterly with every new bit of load that is added, yet you think that the more you carry, the better person you are.** Let's end this dilemma right here. There is nothing to carry, and you don't get any better than you are. You are what you are, and you are not in jeopardy of finding out who that is. You have been a little like the audience who cries all the way through a comedy. Between now and when we talk next, I invite you not only to take in the show, laughing at the humor and the tragedy, but also to become part of the show, or the whole show, as you increase and decrease both the size and number of your perspectives. Have fun and play.

6

The three little kittens washed their mittens
and hung them up to dry.
Oh Mother Dear, see here see here.
We have washed our mittens.
What! Washed your mittens you good little kittens!
But I smell a rat close by.
Mew mew. Hush. I smell a rat close by.

With stories read and both children asleep, I leaned back in my easy chair and began sorting out some of my thoughts. Talking to God seemed to be bringing out the philosopher in me.

"What! Lost your mittens? You naughty kittens. Then you shall have no pie (not die)." I was beginning to notice some of the illusions I had accepted as true. Even in the fairy tales I read to Emily and Judson, there were both suggestive and obvious lessons to learn, and not necessarily lessons I want my children to learn. Authors, directors, actors and speakers can seldom go beyond their own limitations. So, combined within the content of daily reading, watching and listening, we are exposed to the limitations of others. There may be lessons to learn from others and from history, but who determines which ones get passed on and which ones get passed over? There may be lessons from others and from history **not** to learn. If time exists, then we have a heritage which influences us. Even without time, we are influenced by others. If death is really a habit, what other habits do we have without even knowing we do? What am I teaching my children that I don't even know I am teaching them? What am I teaching my wife, and what is she teaching me? What do I cause? What might I be effecting?

I began to realize that questioning my basic assumptions produced interesting and atypical thoughts. The idea of time offers a consistency of thought, but with that consistency comes influence and the temptation to be more effect than cause. I am not sure that this matters, but it might. The degree to which I am programmed by what I perceive to be the past certainly would cramp or entirely determine my style in the present. What should I do? I am confused.

Me: God, I know You say we can't do anything and that we also can't help but do things and that what we do doesn't matter, but in light of all that, **what ought we to do?**

God: What would you do if you painted yourself into a corner? Notice, by the way, that painting is just more doing. So, you find yourself painted into a corner. What do you do?

Me: I can see You are going to have me answer my own question. If I found myself painted into a corner, it would be time to make some decisions. I could remain in the corner until the paint dried. I could back out of my predicament, covering my tracks as I went. I could walk out of the corner and leave tracks that I could always follow if I wanted to get back. Or I could walk out, making tracks, and just leave the tracks there to remind me of the time I painted myself into the corner and walked out. That seems to about cover my options, not counting the more unlikely ones like flying out of the corner or cutting a trap door through the wall or just thinking myself out of the corner in such a convincing manner that I really am out.

God: Very effective analysis. I just wanted to hear you think. You have not painted yourself into a real corner, just an illusionary one, and the easiest way out of an illusionary corner is an illusionary solution. **If you use real measures to get out of a corner that you are not in, you may end up in a real corner.** Ironically, the temptation and ease of doing things within an illusion seems to be so great for people that they don't even attend to where they really are.

So, you want to know what you should do?

Me: Yes, that would make what I do easier.

God: Do you think so?

Me: Yes.

God: Let's talk a little more about how things are for you before we get into specifically what you should do. With any luck at all, this explanation of what human beings think they are in relation to what they really are will make what you ought to do so obvious that you won't need me to tell you.

Me: That makes sense to me.

God: Would you rather be happy or sad?

Me: Happy.

God: Would you rather be a king or a peasant?

Me: A king.

God: Are you ever sad?

Me: Yes.

God: Then it seems that since you say you would rather be happy but that sometimes you are sad, there must be a gap between what you say and what you do.

Me: That seems obvious.

God: If there is a gap between what you say and what you do, then you have a problem of trust. Do you trust what you say or what you do?

Me: I am not sure. I guess I trust what I say sometimes and what I do at other times.

God: So, you can't tell which you will trust because sometimes you trust what you say and sometimes you trust what you do. It seems obvious from my lack of any specific perspective that you always do what you do and that you always say what you say, but that you only sometimes do what you say or say what you do.

Me: I think that is accurate.

God: The game is not to do what you do since that is already accomplished, nor is the game to say what you say because that you have handled. The game is to do what you say and to say what you do.

Me: If You say so. I follow Your reasoning, but I get the sensation of being painted into a corner.

God: I assure you that I am not painting at all; I am just attempting to reveal some whitewashing that you have done without knowing it.

Your game is to say what you are doing and to do what you are saying, so you can no longer say that you want to be happy. You can say that sometimes you want to be happy and sometimes you want to be sad. Sometimes you want to suffer, and sometimes you pretend you don't want to suffer even when you are suffering. When you want to suffer and are suffering, you suffer more easily than when you are suffering and say you don't want to be suffering.

Me: This all seems about as clear as mud but I think You are right. I can't understand it because it is so much a part of what I do that it eludes me.

God: That's right. To **say** what you **do** is putting the cart behind the horse, and it requires you to observe in the present without too much judgment. Let's try a little experiment to get this point across.

Sit down!

Me: I am sitting.

God: I know.

Now sit down.

Me: I am sitting. Oh, I get it—I don't have to say that I am sitting. My sitting is my sitting without me saying anything.

God: Yes.

Now sit down.

Me: (I remain sitting.)

God: So, you are doing what you are doing. Now tell me what you are doing.

Me: I am sitting.

God: Yes. Anything else?

Me: I am breathing, I am thinking, my blood is flowing, my hair is growing and many more biological things are happening.

God: You get no argument from me there.

Do you want to be sitting?

Me: That is a different sort of question. Whether I want to be sitting or not has a different kind of flavor to it than what I am doing. I can want to sit or not want to sit; that is up to me. I can want to sit at one moment and then not want to sit in the next moment and still be sitting the whole time. **I am having fun now.**

God: You have control, at least more control, over what you say or what you think than what you do. You can only want what you want when you want it, but you can change what you want more easily and with less physical variation than changing your position of sitting, say, to a position of standing.

Me: Yes, this is now becoming obvious. **Doing and saying are very different, and I often act as if they are the same thing.** I even act as though what I say or think is more important than what I do. There is usually a rift between what I say and what I do and between what I say and what is. If I had a nickel for every time I said something was the case when it was not, I would have a lot of money now.

God: The money would not matter nearly as much as would closing the gap between what you do and what you say and what you say and what you do. Saying what you do is a simple way of remaining in the present. Doing what you say is the source of the only **possibility of trust** for people. The former is much easier than the latter, not in fact but because of the predicament you find yourself in. From where you are or perceive yourself to be, if I were you, I would first play a bit at determining what you do and saying what you do. After some practice with that, you can venture into doing what you say.

The gap between what you say and what you do creates the foundation for an illusion. Your kingdom is built on illusion wherein you get to be king. Outside of illusion you get to play God, though from within the illusion it doesn't look like it. In your illusionary kingdom, you constantly miss the obvious for the practical and habitual.

Would you rather be happy or sad?

Me: I guess I want to be happy sometimes and sad other times.

God: Would you rather have great sex or mediocre sex?

Me: It seems that I want a mix of the two, with about the same amount of each.

God: With practice, saying what you do will become easier and more obvious. **You will create less confusion and you will be more confused.** You will be confused by things that are really confusing rather than having to manufacture confusion, or anything else, for that matter. This very simple exercise of saying what you do is a first, and a big, step toward **amusement enhancement** without props like that new car, a different spouse, a bigger house or a pony.

Me: Again, I find myself saying that things can't be this easy. Yet I now find myself arguing within myself because they **can** be this easy. I can't make up my mind.

God: Do you have to make up your mind? It seems that it is already always made up.

Me: Could be.

God: It seems that people have forgotten that I have a sense of humor. I made you, didn't I? In my name you get more serious and have less fun than you might without me. If you ever wonder about my sense of humor, look at a Toucan's beak or a Platypus; watch a penguin walk, a frog croak or a person think. **Humor is all around you, and all around you is humor.** Remember certainty comes just before a fall, then seriousness sets in and stays for a while after a fall.

In your world, everything is a matter of perception, perspective and thought. What do you think about that?

Me: Who cares?

God: Exactly. You are blessed. You have been provided with a source of endless entertainment — yourself. There is no better joke than the opportunity to observe oneself with affection and love and without judgment or bias.

Me: Referring to an earlier comment of Yours, it seems that You are saying I might not have free choice. Choice is not something I want to give up just yet.

God: Too late: you have already given it up. The only place that you can even approximate free choice is in a world of illusion. **One of the first illusions you must give up to exit an illusion is free choice.**

Me: I get a bit confused when You use the words "illusion" and "illusions" in the same sentence.

God: I apologize. **Free choice is an illusion.**

Me: What if I don't choose to accept that?

God: You don't have any choice.

Me: I wish I did.

God: You are contradicting our earlier work. A **wish** is a **want**, so I suggest that for your own sake you wish what is instead of wishing for what isn't. You don't have free choice, so you may as well wish that you don't have free choice.

Me: I don't like that very well.

God: There's another great example of a human creating suffering by resisting what is. You don't like it, yet you have no free choice. You may as well like not having it.

Me: I get it.

God: So, back to that lack of free choice of yours . . . that's a joke.

Me: I have noticed that You usually make a joke right after You have taken something away that is really important to me. Do You think that is funny?

God: **I can only take away what you don't have. I can only give you what you already have.** You might want to call me an illusion buster.

You don't have any choice about what you do or think. If you did have a choice, you could sometimes do what you don't do or not do what you do.

Me: I think You are confusing this issue. I could go to the mall or I could stay home; surely that is my choice.

God: Yes, you can go to the mall or you can stay home, but you cannot do both; you must do one or the other. You will only do the one that you do; you will not do the other one. To say you could do either demands a future, which requires time, and we have already busted the illusion of time.

Me: I understand what You are saying, but I am much more comfortable when I think I have free choice.

God: I don't think you mean **comfortable** as much as you mean **typical**. Confusing comfortable and typical can have you repeat the same painful experience many times. Human beings think that just because everybody does something and that it has been done before, then it is worth doing. **Free choice is a Pandora's box.** The moment you perceive the illusion of free choice, you might make the **right** choice or the **wrong** choice. This splitting the world into two camps (the good and the bad, the right or the wrong) is like splitting atoms. When you split atoms, you get a gigantic explosion and with it extensive damage and radioactivity which remains dangerous for years (perhaps an indication that splitting them is not a good idea). **Free choice splits your whole world** and results in repercussions which are much more devastating than splitting atoms. With the illusion of free choice, you become not only the most oppressed species on the planet, but the loneliest. Free choice separates and alienates you from everything and everyone, but it also separates you from yourself. The fallout of this illusion robs you of life and love and lasts for a long time. The illusion of free choice makes you careful, which is something that I never intended you to be. It oppresses you from within and without. It has you attempt to control what you do — a futile effort. It also results in distrust and blame. You don't have free choice, and when you say you do, it is a lie — a very oppressive lie.

Me: I think I understand what You are saying, though I don't think I ought to. Religions have used free choice to oppress people for years, and our whole justice system is based on it. In order to instill a fear of punishment or a fear of the loss of freedom, a person must consider him or herself free. In the punishment alone, we reveal the fact that the person is not free.

God: I couldn't have said it better myself.

Me: So, we are not free. Freedom is an illusion. Free choice not only doesn't exist, but we should thank our lucky stars (or You) that it doesn't.

God: You are welcome. Sometimes you doubt me, but I assure you that **everything has already worked out**.

Me: Strangely enough, that is comforting. **With the loss of free choice, I seem closer to freedom than at any time since I was a small child.**

God: I told you things were funny. You give up free choice and you get freedom. Isn't that a riot?

Me: So if there is no free choice, then there is nothing to worry about.

God: Nothing, or everything, depending on your perspective.

Me: Does that mean I won't worry?

God: No, you will worry when you worry and not worry when you don't worry.

Me: That is what I want.

God: Congratulations. Continually change what you want to what you have and you will arrive where you aren't going before you ever leave. When you don't leave, you can relax and have a good time. It has been a pleasure talking to you. My pleasure. Good-bye for now, and I'll speak with you when I speak with you and not when I don't.

7

Another month went by before God and I spoke again. It was early April and the transformation of winter to spring had begun. I, in my arrogant way, was noticing that perhaps God was right about a few things.

I realized that we do what we do and we don't do what we don't do. We think what we think and we don't think what we don't think. This new philosophy influenced me deeply. I go for walks when I go for walks, and that is nearly every day in the spring.

Emily was growing rapidly. She and I took a walk together to celebrate the end of winter. The smells were beyond compare. While I walked Emily was growing in her stroller. After about an hour of pointing and smiling, noticing and nodding, Emily fell asleep and our walk was concluded. Carefully, I carried her from the stroller to her crib. She certainly weighed more than she used to. I thought about my relationship with Emily and with all people. I wondered whether to trust my thoughts or not.

Me: I think we should talk about truth.

God: Should? According to whom? People keep wrestling with the issue of authority. You should do this and you ought not to do that. This is the right thing and that is the wrong thing. This is the good and that the bad. Relax; take it easy. We don't "should" anything.

Me: I admit it: authority bothers me. Well, not exactly bothers me, but I am almost always trying to act in accordance with one authority or another.

God: You can take it from me, THE FINAL AUTHORITY, there is **no** authority. Remember, I am the one who told you that doing anything isn't really worthwhile, but you still pretend there is something you should do. This is the most basic kind of oppression, and it has gone far enough. **You are not free,** you never were, so you cannot be oppressed. You have to have been free at some point in order to be oppressed — and you have been neither free nor oppressed. You do what you do and you don't do what you don't do. It is not a question of what you **should** do — you can't do other than what you do. I apologize for the simplicity in what I am saying. I am even beginning to confuse myself. The simpler things are, the less thought one needs to have about them. Thus any thought at all is liable to confuse the issue. The absence of oppression and the fact that you do what you do and don't do what you don't do is so simple that it requires the tiniest bit of observation to verify it, and no thought at all.

Me: Are You saying that we **shouldn't** think about it?

God: No, I am saying that when you do think about it, the only thing that you can do with thought is provide **artificial confusion**. There are some ideas that contain no confusion of their own — they are just simple. These ideas are often biological, but not always. There are ideas that people keep saying in different ways because they keep stumbling across them in different locations. A study of some "honest" thinkers, people who were thinking for pure pleasure and curiosity, such as Plato, Shakespeare, Asimov, Leary, Rajneesh and hundreds of others, would provide you with so much similarity of thoughts that you could conclude that those similarities are everywhere. People keep coming up with the same sorts of theories and saying them in different ways.

The truth, at the level that you can understand it, is all around you like the very air you breathe. You are polluting the air and you are polluting the truth as well. It has gotten to the point where getting fresh air takes a lot of searching and breathing. It now, also, takes a lot of thinking to sort through the **craziness, smoke** and **cultural density** to get to the truth. To be a philosopher on Earth, you must almost turn your back on the direction that the general population is going. People always seem to be chasing their tails, an activity which puts them closer to where they have been than where they are going. The dizziness that ensues from tail chasing affects all cultural directions.

Me: Based on our past discussions, I guess I would expect You to say that the truth is simple and that we can see it if we want to.

God: That is what I am saying, but I would not restrict truth to seeing. There is truth in a Beethoven symphony and in the Tschaikowsky Violin Concerto in D major. There is truth in a tree, a frog, and a parent holding a child. There is truth in anything that is and everything that isn't. This truth is always beautiful and inspiring to anyone who can perceive it. The truth is the truth until it is perceived. As a human being, you can be inspired and delighted by the simplest things or by nothing at all, but you often forget how to be. When you are perceptive of yourself and your surroundings, the truth cannot evade you, nor can you evade the truth. There is nothing but truth, yet, through your powers of limitation, you can miss it. I did not design the truth to be shrouded in effort and struggle, restricted to a mountain top, kept in a cave in Tibet or saved for a religious figure to dole out. The truth is yours — it was given to you and given to Earth. Every species knows the truth. Every aspect of the universe, alive or not, is part of the truth.

Me: So the truth is everywhere and we often miss it. How do we go about missing it?

God: Have you ever looked for something very hard, only to find that it was right in front of you the whole time?

Me: Certainly. I could even say I have done that often.

God: Watching you, I could say you do that all the time. The harder you try to find something and the longer you look for it, the more certain you become that it is truly lost. This is the case with the truth on Earth. For generations you have prized the truth, talking about it as if it were a limited thing, a precious commodity. It is **precious, but not limited**. People sell their own truth and use their lack of perception of the truth to oppress other people. The claim by one person that he or she knows the truth and that others do not is the creation of a marketable commodity. Truth, on Earth, is everywhere. Yet you have built an economy based on falsehoods you call truth. For Lord's sake, you teach your children that they cannot know the truth when they already do. Isn't that ironic? You are born knowing and perceiving the truth, both within yourself and outside yourself. It takes years of deception and education before you teach a child to see only your mock truths (illusions) and to distrust him or herself enough to miss the obvious truth all around.

Me: You paint a bleak picture of what we are doing. Is it really that bleak?

God: I don't paint a bleak picture; I only report on the picture. There are still isolated tribes of people on your planet who play every day. These people see the truth.

They are relaxed and comfortable. They have no cancer, no stress, no psychotherapists and virtually no rules. They live each moment as it comes and trust the truth of Earth. They nurture Earth and it nurtures them.

Me: It sounds as though You are saying we should return to being savages.

God: It would sound that way. Can you imagine that God would tell people to return to being savages?

Me: I admit it surprised me.

God: **I am pointing out that you have become savages and that you neither used to be nor need to be.** You only have to read the newspaper or watch the evening news to realize that you are acting like savages.

I gave you the present of selfishness. And, in the name of escaping this selfishness, which you have decided is "bad," you have developed all kinds of heartless, bodiless and empty institutions. You use these institutions, in the name of helping people, to oppress people. You have institutionalized falsehood, which was the only way to inflict your crazy doctrine on so many people.

Me: What, specifically, do You mean by falsehood?

God: You have taught people that they need help. You have taught people that they must work and that their self worth is derived from what they do or what they own. You have convinced people that some of them are "A" students while others are "C" students or worse. You have, in short, set up scales of comparison which make most people look mediocre, a few look superior and a few look special (your new term for the under-achievers). None of these scales measure anything real or of value because your institutions always turn their backs on variation and pretend to be interested in that which can be standardized. You don't think that it is possible to measure anything of value, which is one of your biggest falsehoods. You say that an "A" is better than a "C," but it isn't. Your "A" students don't even do better later in life by your own standards: studies have shown that "C" students outperform "A" students in later life, but you don't seem to notice these studies. You work so hard to create value when it takes no work at all.

Me: I don't like what You are saying and wish You would be a bit nicer.

God: I am not being unkind. I am just pointing out what you have done. You have set up a world of false standards which most people cannot attain. Those who do reach the top will readily admit that there is nothing there worth attaining, only an increase of falseness and hollowness. I am trying to point out to you in the nicest way I know that people are not happier today than they were twenty or a hundred years ago. **You are raising what you call the standard of living without increasing the quality of life.** To increase the quality of life, you only have to see what is around you and rejoice. As a selfish society, your attempts to both help and compete against others are producing a climate in which few, if any, people are happy, and you can only celebrate from time to time, based on circumstances outside yourself.

Earth is a celebration. You are designed to spend your lifetime celebrating. When you are not celebrating, not having fun, not being amused, not enjoying yourself, you are missing the point, off the mark and sinning. I am a little hesitant to say this to you since you have attained the prominent position of falsehood where celebrating can look like having a beer, a new sexual partner, or a political victory. What I mean by celebration is the delight a young child takes in the simplest thing, the feeling a person gets taking a deep breath of fresh air, that pleasant sensation after a walk in the woods or cuddling with someone you love, the thrill of seeing a sunset or a sunrise or romping in the rain. In simple things you can still find the truth and the celebration. It is easy, simple and true.

Me: I understand what You are saying, but there is just too much for me to do. If I am going to put food on the table for my family and have the kinds of things we want and need, I have responsibilities I must fulfill.

God: Listen to what you are saying. In very simple terms you seem to be saying that you need to maintain the craziness or you will not continue to be crazy. This I would agree with, but I don't think you know that that is what you are saying. You have progressed so far that your accomplishments seem to contradict themselves. I am not against your progress. Everything I am suggesting that you celebrate can be celebrated from where you are. You don't need to sell your house and use the money to buy or build a cabin in the woods. I am suggesting no such thing. A fancy house or a good job does not oppress you — they can't. It is you who oppresses you, and I am suggesting that in your own mind you trade that oppression for equal amounts of appreciation. You might even discover that you get more appreciation than you bargained for, since appreciation is natural to you and oppression is not.

Me: I am pleased to hear that You are not saying I have to change my lifestyle.

God: Do not change anything. Most of your problems come from attempts to change things or force adaptation. This is what got you into trouble in the first place. It is the lack of doing that can get you out of it. Please don't change a thing as a result of our conversation, other than your perspective. If you find yourself taking delight in the shape of a snowflake or a cloud formation, then our talk has been worthwhile. You will never be in a more beautiful and wonderful place than you are now; enjoy it. It is not necessary for you to ever delay gratification. There is **everything in anything**. So you never need to find yourself lacking. If you think you are lacking, it is that delusion that is the problem. To take care of the delusion, all you need to discover is the enjoyment that resides within you. It is there — your joy can't leave. I put it there and it remains, neglected.

Me: So, if satisfaction, delight and happiness are within me, I shouldn't have to work so hard to get them.

God: Yes, these are not virtues that you work for; they are who you are. You must turn your back on who you are to be unhappy, unsatisfied or suffering. The greater your suffering, the more completely you have forgotten who you are. By your very nature you are a creature of celebration. This is something you cannot change no matter how hard you try. Your ability to celebrate is independent of your number of promotions, the size of your wardrobe, your IQ and your wallet.

Me: Again, You seem to be throwing out what is most important to me. It sounds like You are anti-American.

God: I am not anti-American. You can't blame a compass for pointing north or a thermometer for reporting the correct temperature. You may not like its findings, but the purpose of the thermometer is to indicate the temperature. If the thermometer was stuck at 72 degrees, regardless of the temperature, you would become upset with the thermometer, call it broken and throw it out. If you didn't realize that the thermometer was broken, you would attempt to ignore changes in temperature, thinking that it was 72 degrees because that is what the thermometer said. It would take extreme changes of temperature, changes so big that you could not ignore them, for you to question the thermometer. Your scales of measure are broken, and you have reduced variation or ignored variation so thoroughly that you don't notice. Your psychology is built on the prototype cultural human being who is a bit nutty. If you develop dog psychology based on a dog on a leash, you will miss much of what it is to be a dog. You have developed your psychology based on people in culture, which is a bit like being on a leash. In their attempt to standardize and control, people have tried to keep everything consistent within society, but, like the thermometer that remains consistent in the face of variation, they are of little use to each other.

You no longer report on what is; you report on what you think should be or ought to be. You have settled for appearances, and settling makes you shallow and hollow. You say that things are one way when, in fact, they are not that way at all, this misinterpretation has resulted in distrust of yourself and each other. You have turned from being a creature of trust and celebration to being a creature of rules and oppression. You squeeze all the truth out of life and then mourn and suffer because you can't find it anymore. You would have to notice yourself squeezing out the truth to notice that you were not able to really squeeze it out. This awareness is an effective first step to seeing the truth.

Me: I think I am getting a lecture which I don't want, but which, perhaps, I need. You seem to be telling me that I must take my medicine although it will taste bitter.

God: I am telling you that you have been taking your

medicine right along in ever-increasing dosages and have become an addict without even knowing what you are taking.

Me: I understand. The last thing an alcoholic wants to hear is that he or she is an alcoholic, but hearing it and admitting it is the first step to recovery.

God: Yes. People have become creatures of the quick fix — busy trying to do the right thing and carry their fair share. You are doing all the wrong things for all the right reasons, and your lives are getting worse. There was a time when a good day's work meant a good night's rest, but no more. There was a time when people earned something and were proud of what they earned. Now the earning goes on without pride. There is nothing of value that you can earn. Real value is within you and all around you and only needs to be noticed, not earned.

Me: You seem to keep saying the same thing to me in different ways and sometimes in the same way. I think I am beginning to understand. If I smile a bit more at nothing, I have done my part.

God: I like the "smile a bit more," but there is no part for you to do. There is no you apart from everything and everyone else, and there is no part for you to "do." What separates **apart** from **a part** is a space, but the meanings are very different. Meaning is strange and untrustworthy. **If you give meaning a little space, it can change to its opposite.**

You can perceive the whole, but not through doing. **I made Earth big enough to play in and too big to control.** There is not even a niche small enough to control or too small to play in. If you are not big enough to push over a tree, you might want to appreciate the tree in its upright position. If you keep trying to push it over, you will wear yourself out. If you design a machine to push the tree over, you lose touch with and appreciation for the tree. Since you and the tree are not separate, you lose touch with yourself at the same time.

I have been a little hard on you during this meeting. I sounded a bit like a preacher, and I apologize. It is not your thinking alone that has gotten you into this fix, but it is your thinking and celebrating that can bring you out of it. It has taken years of abuse and disrespect to have the problems you now have. Primarily disrespect for yourself, but for Earth as well. The way out does not take years. It can be done very quickly on the path of happiness. It takes little effort to get out of a predicament that you've been in for years. If this were not the case, you would have to do a lot of work to get out, and doing work would only get you further in.

You might want to view yourself in your predicament like being trapped in a tunnel. You are stuck in this long, dark tunnel created by your current use of thought and by your commitment to seriousness and being right. You can exit the tunnel at any moment. How long you have been inside need have nothing to do with when you find the exit and get out. You consider the tunnel

so important and meaningful that leaving it is both necessary and scary.

Me: So there are ways out of the problems we find our-
selves in?

God: Yes, and, ironically, caring more about the problems and taking them seriously will only drive you
deeper. This is counter-intuitive to your thinking patterns. Seriousness, work and caring, the ingredients
used to get you into this mess, won't get you out. **Lightness, play and selfishness are your keys to getting
out.**

Me: I can't quite believe that God tells me the way out
and I want to argue. Lightness sounds all right, except that I have much more experience with heaviness. Play seems like the wrong thing to do because
I have been taught that work is good and play is something that I earn by working. Selfishness not only
doesn't sound right at all, but it isn't right; it can't be
right. Selfishness is always bad. Everybody knows
that.

God: **If you didn't have the response to the way out
that you do, you wouldn't be in the predicament
you are in.** You are the only species on Earth who will
do what you think is the right thing while disregarding
all evidence to the contrary. **You are turning Earth
into hell both intellectually and physically while
arguing for the progress you are making in this
difficult task.**

We cannot resolve this in conversation. You must discover the resolution through **inaction**. The evidence I again suggest you attend to is whether you are having fun, whether you feel lighter and whether you experience more pleasure in the simplest things. You have been operating with a false sense of security, and you may need to give that up to discover real security. A false sense of security is much more difficult to give up than a real one. Giving up the false security may look threatening when, in fact, it is necessary. I wish you luck with this, and I remind you that it is your thinking and specifically the importance you put on it that has gotten you into trouble. It is the lack of thinking or lack of importance placed on it that will get you out.

On just the other side of heaviness is extreme lightness, but you can't see this light from inside the tunnel. You get the light when you exit the tunnel. If you had to see the light at the end of the tunnel to know which way to go, you would miss the opportunity to trust yourself. Trust yourself — not your thoughts, but yourself. You know the way out of the tunnel.

Thank you for the conversation. Until next time, goodbye.

8

The next night, God and I spoke again. Time and I had been having a new relationship. My ability to be aware had increased so much that it seemed I lived a lifetime in one twenty-four hour period. I was only planning on peeking in to see if Emily was covered when God spoke to me. I was surprised by how much I had to say.

God: Have you noticed anything since we last spoke?

Me: Yes, I have noticed a lot. I have noticed that I often attend to what I want to have happen more than to what is happening. I have also noticed that children always seem to experience each moment. They cry when they cry and laugh when they laugh. They laugh much more than they cry. I kind of cry all the time without ever really showing that I am crying. My suffering is a kind of toned-down crying; my happiness is a short-term break in my crying.

Today I delivered a sales talk that went well, and I got a raise, but I didn't celebrate afterward for nearly as long as I fretted and worried beforehand. I have been noticing what is going on with me and trying not to change things. This seems to have resulted in my having more energy and being happier.

I have still been trying to figure out what will really make me happy.

God: The answer to that is simple: everything and nothing. When you are happy you are happy, and when you are sad you are sad. When you are sad, you look around to find something to blame your sadness on. When you are happy, you look around to find something to attribute your happiness to.

Me: Nothing is really happy or sad?

God: No, you always add the interpretation. Without you, nothing would have any meaning at all. **Without you, the closest anything could get to meaning would be function.** You add judgment to everything, based on your mood, and by doing so, you manufacture meaning and importance. Nothing contains importance intrinsically.

Me: So, there is no such thing as a "good" car or a "good" thing to do? There is no right or wrong? We add all meaning and all value?

God: Yes. If you stopped adding meaning for a little bit, you would discover that there is no such thing as meaning. **Meaning is a form of thought pollution.** Meaning is to thought as leaning is to your body. When you lean on something, you become precarious and dependent on whatever you are leaning on. Similarly, you depend on the thoughts you add meaning to while disliking your position of dependence. When you are dependent, you are susceptible.

Many people have added meaning to physical things: their car, house or boat. Other people add it to their activities: their jobs, housework, hobby or volunteer work. Almost everyone adds meaning to thoughts. Any time you add meaning, you do so to make yourself important, implying that you were not important without the meaning. Meaning is more addictive than any drug. Using a tool or an occupation to prove that you are important is addictive and leads to dependence and insecurity.

You have a boat and your neighbor does not, so surely you are more important than your neighbor, right? You don't often say this directly, but it is in your thoughts. You have a boat, so you must be good, successful or important. It is hard to find the time to go out in your boat because you are so busy paying for it, but finally you make boating your priority. The moment you are in your boat, you are tense and upset. Your boat is a symbol of your success, a very fragile symbol at that. You hit a rock, and rather than laugh, you get angry and act as though it is you who has been hurt. Every time you place your importance outside yourself, you become vulnerable.

You could have a boat without adding meaning to it, but that is rare. People add meaning to everything and then pretend that the meaning is in the thing, activity, person, thought or place. You have developed a life dependent on symbols and appearances. It is a hollow and lonely life with little satisfaction and tremendous exposure to loss or damage. Fear is the unnatural result of such a life, and fear is one thing you have plenty of.

Me: I am not that scared.

God: Boo! Did you notice the way you jumped when I said boo? It may not be obvious to you that you are scared, but it is obvious to me. Your fear does not always look like fear; it masquerades as other emotions. Anger is another face of fear, as is sadness, and, in your culture, so is love. You have invented other emotions to cover up your fear. You don't want yourself or anyone else to recognize your fear, so you cover it up. A person gets angry and yells at her spouse — out of fear. A person gets sad when someone near to him appears to die — again out of fear. You even think emotions mean something. They don't. Emotions are just reminders of your humanness; they always tell you when it is time to let go. You fall in love, meaning it is time to let go of whomever it is that appears to be the object of that love.

A baby knows how to grasp and has to learn how to release things. If you want to discover life without fear, you must learn to let go in the face of any emotion.

Me: It seems that You are saying I should not care about anything. I hold on to people because I love and care for them.

God: No, you hold on to a person to reduce fear in yourself. I am not suggesting that you don't care because basically you are a creature who cares. I am suggesting that holding too tightly to anything results in your having emotions, which is always a sign that you ought to let go; you are taking something or someone much too seriously.

I am not saying you have to leave the person you love. I am saying you must not hold on to her. When you hold tightly to something, your grasp becomes of utmost importance and the object you are holding is lost to you. In loosening your grasp, you will discover much more about your object of importance.

Seeing an animal in the zoo is not like seeing that animal in the wild. The smaller the cage, the less the caged animal represents its wild counterparts. You lock up what you own in an effort to protect it. You put together your own collection of things that have meaning to you and then expend effort to protect them. Everybody on the planet and even the family dog becomes a threat to the things you own. The dog could chew up your favorite shirt. If it is something you like very much, a thing of great value, a jewel, perhaps, you lock it in the smallest box and put it in the safest place you know of and still you can't enjoy it. You worry about someone breaking into your safe and taking it.

I made you **selfish**, but I did not make you **possessive**. I made you selfish so you could look out for yourself. I never considered that you would miss who you are so completely that you would confuse yourself with your boat, house, car, job, relationship or baseball card collection. I created you and then let you go. If I held you tightly, I would not be following my own advice. You have to learn to let go so that you can get on with living. You have so many other things to learn and your own pace to keep up with.

Me: So You say we have to learn to let go and that emotions let us know when to do so. Is there anything we should hold on to? I'm asking for help here; I want a little reassurance.

God: You could always hold your own hand.

Me: There You go taking away all that I add meaning to and then making a joke about it.

God: It isn't a joke. I gave you two hands for obvious useful reasons, but also as a joke, so you would have a constant reminder of where you are: right and left. But most of all I gave you two hands so that you could hold your own hand. If you find yourself holding too tightly, you will be the first to know it. If you let go of your own hand, you will notice that, too. I have given you a body you can hold on to, but you can also notice the repercussions of holding it too tightly.

To put it simply, **anything worth holding on to is worth letting go of. The very act of holding and**

then letting go is the essence of learning. When you hold without releasing, you stop learning and start defending. When what you know becomes more important than what you can learn, you circle the wagons and begin to defend what you know. While you are holding, you aren't learning. I gave you two sets of muscles in each part of your body, one for holding and one for releasing. If you apply this wisdom of the body to the mind, you will learn rapidly enough that fear will become a thing of the past.

Me: Will You repeat that last statement?

God: **If you apply this wisdom of the body to the mind, you will learn rapidly enough that fear will become a thing of the past.**

Me: I think that is one of the most important things I have ever heard.

God: Watch out. There you go making something important again. Telling someone that she just said one of the most important things you have ever heard could flatter her to the extent that she may attempt to identify herself with what was just said and then hold on.

Temptation is everywhere, but it is nowhere **less obvious** than in your thoughts. **Nothing that you think is important.** Yet one of the ways you cause problems for yourself is to think that your thoughts are more important than anything else. People break up marriages, pollute Earth and even kill others over ideas and thoughts. If you are on a cliff, falling, and you grab a tree branch, you may stop your fall, but holding on to an idea just stops an imaginary fall and robs you of an imaginary landing. One consequence of this holding on to thoughts is that you are left constantly up in the air with no solid footing and no ground to stand on. **Manufactured uncertainty is the major by-product of thought. When you add meaning to thoughts, you add meaning to nothing (with the thought that you are adding meaning to something). This is illusion.** This process is the root of all your problems and suffering.

Me: How can I learn to let go?

God: First by noticing that you are holding on to something and then by opening up wherever you are closed. Openness, the opposite of holding, is the door, flexibility is the key, and inside is self-esteem. What you do or what you own is not important until you make it important. Making something important requires you to become less flexible, increases threats and broadens the area that you must defend.

You let go by letting go. Practice by starting with small things. Pick up an orange and then let it go. Pick up a pencil and then let it go. Pick up a quarter and then let it go. Pick up a diamond and then let it go. Give someone you don't know a twenty dollar bill. Continue to practice holding and then releasing, working up to bigger and bigger things until you can have a thought and let it go. Practice until you can have the "right" thought and then let it go. During this whole process you will learn and you will grow. Hold on to the learning and then let it go. One strange thing you will discover is that some of what you hold on to the tightest is the most illusionary. Illusion requires a good bit of holding, the tighter the better.

Me: Again this sounds simple. You have taken the complex and made it sound simple.

God: You have made it complex, and I just reminded you that it is simple. I have revealed what is really there.

Everything is simple. Any time it appears to be complex, you or some other person has been up to **meaning-full mischief** again. Hold on and let go. That is what you were designed for. You have habits of holding and never letting go or of trying not to hold at all. Habits take practice to implement and a moment to break. Break these habits and you will grow and learn very rapidly. The holding and then letting go are of equal importance — no importance. The moment you treat them as such, life will again become playful for you.

Me: Would it be all right if I held on to a few things? I don't want to let my job go . . . or my new brown shoes.

God: It is all right if you don't let anything go, but remember what you don't let go of becomes a source of fear for you rather than enjoyment. You can hold on to something and apparently restrict its flexibility, but at the same time, you restrict your own. It is important for growth and learning that you let go of what you most want to hold on to. The more valuable something is to you, the more beneficial it will be to let go of it. You can appreciate a songbird, but if you hold it too tightly it won't sing, and it may never sing again.

Me: I don't like it, but I know You are right. Earlier this year two birds hit our window and fell to the ground. Judson gently picked them up, putting one in each hand, and noticed that they were still breathing. After about a half hour of holding them, the one in his left hand started to move, and within moments it flew. I do not have words to describe the look on my son's face when the bird flew—it was a look of such extreme delight. It took another five minutes for the second bird to fly. My son had held the birds and let them go. In that experience he gained more appreciation for both the birds and himself than I think he ever had before. It was a demonstration of holding, letting go and pleasure. He could have caged the birds and kept them around for years, but he would have missed the pleasure and learning of letting them go. The birds in a cage might have become his, but they would have ceased to be themselves.

God: I could not have said it better myself. It is not what you hold on to, but how you hold on to it and how you release it. The holding and releasing are the keys to pleasure.

Me: I guess this would work with everything, wouldn't it?

God: Of course, things are not as separate and distinct as they appear. What I tell you will work with everything **because everything is the same.**

Me: I am not sure how this applies to my spouse. Do I have to let my spouse go?

God: Yes. Your spouse has to be free to fly. You have the opportunity to hold on to and let go of your spouse each moment. It is this process of alternately holding and releasing each other that nourishes a relationship.

Let's pretend you have a dog and a cat. They co-exist peacefully, often curling up together on the hearth. The dog learns that the cat has claws and the cat learns that the dog just wants a friend. They get along well, until you tie them together. The same cat and dog that used to seek out each other's company will fight tooth and nail when forced to remain together. You and your spouse will display similar behaviors if you use marriage to hold on to each other. You must let each other go (which does not mean leave). It means that you each must be able to leave at every moment. The more you can loosen your hold on your spouse, the more aware you become of your spouse rather than your hold on your relationship. Releasing your spouse re-opens the door of appreciation and discovery. Hold close, tighten your grasp and then let your spouse go. When I say this, it sounds a bit like sex. In and out, up and down, hold and release. The process of life is similar to sex and can be at least as pleasurable as the best sex you can have or imagine.

Me: I am a little uncomfortable with God talking about sex.

God: You are a bit uncomfortable with anyone talking about sex. Lighten up. Hold on and let go.

Me: What You are saying makes sense and I will practice it. It still seems to me that there are certain ideas worth holding on to no matter what. It still seems that there are some ideas that are "right" and some that are "wrong."

God: That is a limitation of your perspective. There is nothing that can't be changed with practice. Holding on and letting go is a matter of technique which can be practiced. As you practice, life may become a source of entertainment and amusement for you again and less of a struggle. People pay for entertainment that they can easily and inexpensively provide for themselves. We could go on, but I think you have enough to practice right now. The more you practice holding on to meaning and then letting it go, the better you will be at thinking. You will **discover** how powerful you are and you won't have to try to **prove** it so often. You will learn that life is a flow for you to dance with and that blocking that flow causes countless problems. Practice and play and enjoy your world.

Me: Thanks. I will, and thank You for our chat tonight.

9

Over the next month and a half I practiced holding on to and letting go of things, thoughts and beliefs, even practicing and letting go of beliefs in God and in myself. I discovered that the longer I held something, the more it meant to me; perhaps time and meaning have some kind of secret pact. I could make anything important — it seemed that the more **insignificant** something was, the more important I made it.

God and I had our next conversation under the stars near Lake Superior while the family was asleep after a long day of hiking and swimming.

God: You take yourself so seriously. You are in danger of extinction from your excessive seriousness.

Me: People do take themselves very seriously, don't they?

God: Yes. It is quite funny. Even when I tell you that you take yourself seriously, you take that seriously.

Me: When I step back and watch myself, it does seem funny, but when I am being serious, humor is very far from my reach.

God: You might want to practice stepping back — viewing yourself and others from a distance. I find that it is very easy to watch people from an infinite distance — one of my perspectives. Closeness often brings a loss of perspective. Problems and solutions look the same from the right distance and appear different from up close. Distance increases the appearance of unity. Bringing unity to closeness is more difficult, but possible.

When an artist paints a picture, its value and worth is not based on his or her subject matter, but on the way the picture was painted. People have an understanding of art that they could bring to the realm of thinking. **How** you think is more important than **what** you think. It is the perspective that you bring to thinking and the way you think that determines the value of your thought. When you believe that your thinking is **real** and **important,** you have to be careful of what you think. This limits your thinking. When you view your thinking as amusing and entertaining, you become flexible and make room for unlimited thinking.

The pleasure you get from thinking is inversely proportional to the importance you place on the content of each thought. The less importance you place on a thought, the more pleasure you get from it. Creativity is a result of pleasure. When you are under the pressure of "important thinking," you become reactionary and lose the ability to be creative.

Given your quantity of thinking, you are certain to increase your amount of fun if you enjoy the process of thinking. Similarly, enjoy breathing since you breathe a lot. The choice to enjoy breathing and thinking is not yours to make. However, with practice you can enjoy and savor every thought and breath. Practice taking each thought more lightly than the one before it.

Me: I heard someone say once that life is empty and meaningless. That was very upsetting to me. As a matter of fact, it still is.

God: Life being meaningless and upsetting to you is a contradiction. If life is really empty and meaningless, then it doesn't mean anything.

Me: I get it. That makes it easier. Is life meaningless?

God: When it is, it is. When it isn't, it isn't.

Me: Again You are saying that it is a matter of my perspective. Is everything dependent on my perspective, or is there really a reality?

God: Isn't it amazing that we have now had numerous chats and you have not asked me about reality? Waiting so long is indicative of either your lack of interest in reality or your thinking that you can't know what reality is. Yes, there is a reality, but it won't do you much good to know what it is. I can tell you what it is, but you won't care for the answer.

Me: I do want to know what reality is. I disagree that it won't do me much good to know what it is. I have always wanted to know what reality is; I just forgot to ask until now. I have been taught that I cannot really know what reality is although I think that I am real and that things are real.

God: It amazes me that I know what reality is, that I know who you are, that I tell you it won't do you any good to know what reality is, and that you disagree with me. You don't have a clue as to what reality is, and you only have vague opinions about who you are. Yet you have the audacity to tell me I am wrong.

Me: I am sorry if I offended You.

God: You don't offend me. You amuse me — again.

Me: Are You going to tell me what reality is? The closest You have come so far is to say that I do what I do and don't do what I don't do. Is that reality?

God: Are you sure you want to know what reality is?

Me: Well, I guess if I wanted to know I would already know, but I am getting more **curious** by the moment.

God: I will not tell you what reality is, but I will tell you enough about it to enable you to figure out what it is.

Let me begin by telling you what reality is not. The simple rule for determining what reality is not is that **REALITY REQUIRES NO MAINTENANCE.**

Anything that needs maintenance has very little to do with reality even though it is influenced by reality, as is everything.

Me: Again, that seems simple. So my house is not real, nor is my boat or even myself. My thoughts seem to require maintenance as do books and television sets. It seems that everything requires maintenance. Are You telling me that there is no such thing as reality?

God: Yes.

Me: I don't think You're right.

God: You said that your house is not real. I am not speaking of what is real; I am speaking of what reality is. There could be an important difference between these two — but there is not.

Me: Are You making another joke as You take my house, car, boat and thoughts away?

God: Yes. There is no such **thing** as reality, but that does not mean that there is not reality — it means that reality is not a **thing**. There is reality. You are always dancing in reality. Reality is the **no-thing** that makes you and everything possible — in fact, reality is just that — **possibility**.

Me: So, if something is possible for me, then it is real?

God: You should enter a long jump competition. That was a marvelous leap you just made.

Reality is not a **some-thing**, it is a **no-thing** (not nothing). What is possible for you is such a small group of possibilities that it doesn't even matter, except to you.

Reality is **all** possibilities. If reality required maintenance, it could end or not be kept up. Reality is simply every possibility, every single one, **ALL**. I don't know how to say it in such a way that you understand the word **ALL**. Every single possibility that ever has been, is or ever will be. **ALL**. Reality is absolute possibility.

Statistics teaches that everything has a probability. Sometimes that probability is so small that it never happens, but it always **could**. Even the least probable event still has some possibility.

Wasn't that a Sopwith Camel that just flew through here? Maybe not, but it is possible that it was. People have eyes for everything, but they learn to attend to only what is most probable. **ALL possibility is infinitely interesting, whereas some possibility is somewhat interesting and one possibility is a problem.** Much of your "work" is geared toward producing and reproducing one possibility — think about that for a while. In statistics as well as in life, there is not zero possibility. Possibilities are endless and infinite, and none of them means anything.

Me: What am I supposed to do with that?

God: I told you that you wouldn't care for my answer about reality. And since there is nothing to do, why should reality concern doing? It doesn't.

You can, however, use the knowledge of what reality is in a practical way. You only get upset or have a problem when you perceive that your possibilities have been limited — either by yourself or by circumstances outside yourself.

For instance, you think getting fired is a problem when you perceive that your possibilities have been limited. In reality, they have not been limited at all. On a quest for control, humans have become fixated on the limitation of possibilities, and they define themselves by illusionary boundaries. **Humans act as though the more possibilities they obscure from themselves, the more secure they are.** But the moment they perceive that a possibility is lost, they act like they have been robbed of something that was near and dear to them.

Possibilities are a constant indication of who you are; the relationship between the possibilities you can perceive and the possibilities there are determines everything you do, everything you think and who you are.

The limitation of possibilities looks like security when it is, in fact, treacherous. What is possible for you? Everything. What do you perceive as possible for you? Very little. The difference between these two is the playground of thought.

Me: Everything is possible for me, but I don't think it is. This is my problem? To some extent, that makes sense to me. I notice that when I think I have to do something, I don't have fun doing it. I call what I have to do work. That is a way of saying that at a particular moment, I only have one possibility. Play is more fun for me because I have more possibilities. I can play in the mall, at the beach, in a park or at home. I can only work at the office. It is not quite as cut and dried as the way I am stating it, but do You get the idea?

God: I do.

Me: It now seems obvious that when I have a problem, I seem to have fewer possibilities. You are saying that I always have all possibilities even when I don't perceive them.

God: Yes, I am saying that you enjoy life most when you perceive more possibilities. The moment you think there are right things to do or right thoughts to have, you limit your perception of possibilities. The moment you **do** anything, you limit your perception of possibilities. The moment you **think** something, you limit the possibilities you are able to perceive.

When you play tennis, you eliminate all possibilities other than tennis. Tennis has certain rules designed to make it replicable and predictable by limiting other possibilities that might arise. You have names for specific sets of limitations, such as tennis, golf, marriage, work, plumber and so on. A plumber does not do open heart surgery, since surgery is beyond the possibilities of the specific set of limitations called a plumber. Children are allowed to laugh on the playground at school, but, if they laugh in class at a particular multiplication problem they find funny, they are liable to be punished. Random laughter is not a possibility included in the specific set of limitations called "order in the class-room." You are told that learning can be fun, but not funny.

People are supposed to keep abreast of the current limitations of possibility in every defined area of life. A dentist now has to wear rubber gloves, at least when she is working on a patient. You can't return a purchase without a receipt. You have rules, laws, ordinances, and things-that-go-without-saying at the level of family, the workplace, community, society and Earth. Staying within every rule, structure and limitation is a full-time job which many people take very seriously at the cost of creativity, pleasure and amusement.

The source of value in doing nothing is that you can perceive more possibilities than you can in doing something. Doing draws your attention away from possibilities. Thinking often draws your attention to the limitation of possibilities, especially serious thinking. Every **thing** vies for your attention. All **things** are the embodiment of frozen possibilities in a specific location. All things are a function of limitations which are perceived differently as their possibilities increase and flow while they thaw out. Everything devolves (evolves) to greater and greater possibility and away from a specific set of possibilities.

Me: I understand what You are saying, but it seems that I shouldn't. You are telling me something I have known all the time but that I didn't know I knew. The obvious becomes evident again, thank God.

God: You are welcome.

Me: I don't want to talk any more right now. I have to think. I have to think about what You just told me. It is so accurate that I can hardly remember it. Can we talk again soon?

God: Of course. Go, think and have fun. We will tie up any loose ends next time we talk. I suspect that your thinking will produce some interesting questions. I am delighted that you want to play this one out on your own. I am always here when you are ready.

10

Reality as possibility was a new idea to me. It was certainly not what I had been taught, but I took to the idea very quickly. I liked the results that came from exploring possibility, and my fears disappeared as I took on more possibilities and perspectives. Since my last conversation with God, I began to notice that I was having spontaneous and unprecedented amounts of fun. I was as curious and happy as a child at the playground. My identity and limitations were beginning to disappear, and sometimes I wasn't sure who I was, but I also wasn't sure who I wasn't. This uncertainty resulted in more play and enjoyment than I thought I deserved.

God: Welcome back. It looks as if you have been having more fun.

Me: I have. It seems like I have been having more fun than I deserve.

God: I doubt that. You deserve a lot of fun, and the more fun you have, the more you deserve. You find out what you deserve by what you get. When I look at people and watch their suffering and struggling, it indicates to me that there is more suffering and struggling to come. Tell me about what you have been **up** to.

Me: I had a fight with my spouse the other day. We have routines like most couples who have been together for a while. We play by a set of unspoken rules. Our fights generally last for about an hour, and we each stay upset for a few hours afterwards; then we settle down. Our last fight was very different from our routine. The whole fight lasted about five minutes and ended with us both laughing so hard we cried. We were laughing at nothing in particular, but we sure had fun.

God: You are learning how to play and find delight in anything. That is a great way to increase your amount of fun. Every evolutionary step can provide an increase in fun and human advancement as well as an increase in the number of problems.

There is a problem with conversation between humans in that people take things one of two ways: as theory or as practice. These two are very different, but the difference disappears when theory masquerades as practice. Often, people have an insight or a novel idea, but they relate to it in theory and neglect to put it into practice.

People know better than to make most of the mistakes

and have most of the problems they have, but they still have them. **Knowing better in your thinking is theory; knowing better in your body and behaving accordingly is practice.** The story about you and your wife lets me know that you are applying what we are talking about practically.

Me: Yes. And I don't even **know** what I am doing or **how** I am applying it, but I like the results.

God: You don't **know** but you still **do**. The nature of thoughts is that they always come along after behaviors and look as if they come before. You can have a routine argument with your spouse even though you know better than to have it. Or you can break up the routine and enter new terrain, independent of your old routines. The process of growth happens first in behaviors and application; then, sometime later, you **may** know what you did. Knowing only has the possibility of doing you some "good" if you use your thinking practically. Nothing does you any "good" if you take your thinking seriously. This is a uniquely human dilemma.

Me: So, thoughts come along after behaviors, not before?

God: Yes. You can think almost anything, but you can only do certain things. Repetitious and habitual behaviors are very rapid. To stand up, you coordinate hundreds of muscles. If you had to think to stand up, you would not be able to do it.

Thought generalizes and, in the process, adds meaning and relevance when there is, in fact, only function. When you think too seriously, function disappears for you and you miss the obvious. You miss what you **are** doing or even where you **are**, while attending to what you **think** you are doing or where you **think** you are.

Your body operates at a much faster pace than does your thinking or knowing. Your brain operates at that faster pace because it is part of your body. **Your mind works at the slower pace because it is a fictitious place where your thoughts become known to you.** When you treat thoughts, the products of your mind, as real, you confuse fiction with nonfiction, slowing yourself down. Your whole busy-ness is a product of your thoughts not being able to keep up with your actions — something they were never intended to do.

Me: This difference in speed makes it obvious why my thoughts are not as important as I sometimes make them. I wouldn't bet on the slowest horse in a race if I wanted to win; I would bet on what I considered to be the fastest horse.

God: Sometimes your behaviors appear even sillier than betting on the slowest horse. Many people pay so much attention to their past and their thoughts that they bet on the horse who has already lost the race. They know the horse has lost the race, but they still think it is the right horse and bet heavily on it.

Me: That seems ridiculous. It is no wonder that people suffer. Betting on a known loser doesn't sound so smart.

God: It isn't too smart, but it does provide something for the person doing the betting. Can you guess what it provides?

Me: Well, what does everybody want and almost nobody have? In a strange way it seems like it provides a sense of security.

God: Right on. It provides the security of knowing the outcome. You can know what will happen, but you usually don't. You think you **know** what did happen, but this knowledge is only a reflection of your limited perspective. **For some people, the only security they have is knowing that they will lose.**

Me: That sounds very bleak, but that is not me—at least not anymore. I would rather have the uncertainty and the chance at winning or losing. Then there is a game.

God: And that is exactly what you do have.

Back to the theoretical and practical for a moment. If people applied **all** they know, the human race would be over; you would have lost the race. You would already be extinct. No wonder people keep moving faster and faster: they think there is a race, the human **race**. Slow down. Smell the roses. There is no race. If people applied **some** of what they know, they would be in deep trouble — and you are. If people applied **none** of what they know, they would be creatures of constant bliss.

Without application, thought could result in amusement.

Once upon a time there was a Russian farmer. A Communist party member came to test the farmer's loyalties. The party member said, "If you had twenty chickens, how many chickens would you have?" The farmer responded very quickly by saying, "I would have ten chickens and the state would have ten chickens." "Very good," said the interviewer. "And if you had ten pigs, how many pigs would you have?" The farmer solemnly replied, "I would have five and the state would have five." "Again that is correct," said the man representing the state. "If you had four cows, how many cows would you have?" This time the farmer took several minutes to respond and appeared to be deep in thought. Finally he answered, **"But I have four cows."**

This little story illustrates the difference between **practical** and **theoretical**. Virtually everything your government is based on is theoretical and, as such, it mirrors the people well because most people live in a world of theory. **Theory should at best be fun and entertaining. But, due to the slow nature of thought, its application is problematic and incomplete, and it requires struggle and effort while confusing what is with what isn't.** Possibility is. And what isn't is all the things and ideas you consider to be important. Theory is always about illusion. Reality does not care about theory. Theory requires much more care and maintenance than even the more obvious illusions around you like cars, boats and houses. Theory must be carried all of the time; it has no ability to walk or move on its own. If it is not carried or sustained by someone, it disappears. Theory requires constant maintenance. Theory appears to be the leader when it is, in fact, the follower. The caboose does not lead the train, does not have the ability to drive itself and has no power or energy of its own other than that provided for it by the engine. Your theories and thoughts are the caboose, reality is the engine and you are in one of the passenger cars. You can enjoy the ride, worry about the destination, celebrate each moment or complain about the conditions and the scenery.

Me: I think I am enjoying the ride more than ever before. I have You to thank for that. Thank You.

God: You are welcome. You also have you to thank for that because you couldn't have done it without yourself. One form of celebration that is always available to you is to congratulate yourself for whatever is happening to you and whatever you are thinking at the moment.

The more you accept and even celebrate where you are and what you are thinking, the more possibilities you can perceive — thus, the closer you are to reality. The more you resist your circumstances and thoughts, the fewer possibilities you can perceive and the more you are forced into a corner where all escape is illusionary, as is the corner. You create the illusion, and then anything that looks the slightest bit like an increase in possibilities becomes a threat.

Me: I like the **reality route** better, along with its inherent increase in possibilities.

God: You can like it better now. We have done enough damage to some of your illusions that it seems worthless to rebuild them. You can dance with reality or suffer through illusion; you are now doing more dancing and less suffering. Congratulations.

Me: Thank You. It still seems strange to celebrate where **I am** with whatever is happening to me, but it makes sense. I was taught from a very early age not to have too much fun or enjoy my own company. That teaching has stuck with me until recently. How did our society get into this mess?

God: Basically by thinking that your thinking is more important than anything else. You have trusted your thinking to evaluate itself; as with all self-fulfilling prophecies, thinking reached the conclusion that it was important.

A group of kindergartners, when asked to evaluate their own drawings, will all conclude that they are artists. Most adults, on the other hand, when asked to evaluate their own drawings, will admit with some embarrassment that they don't draw well. The difference between these two groups is that the adults think more of their thinking and judge themselves into unimportance by making things meaningful. Ironic, isn't it?

You have noticed that as you become amused by your thinking, you have more fun, and so do the people around you. You even get more done with less work or effort. As a child, you built a tree house. Remember that?

Me: How could I forget? I enjoyed that tree house more than I now enjoy my expensive suburban home or my condominium in the Fiji Islands.

God: In your tree house, you played. You always did what you wanted to do. Building the tree house was not work for you — it was play. Anything appeared possible in your tree house. Your imaginary relationships with your imaginary friends were more real than many of your friendships now. You knew these were illusions while acting as though they were not. As you grew, you left those imaginary friends behind and built bigger and supposedly better illusions, but you forgot that they were illusions. You can return to those days of play simply by recognizing illusion for what it is and constantly increasing your possibilities.

When your tree house had a hole in the roof, that meant that you got to fix it. When your house has a hole in the roof, that means that the rain might come in and ruin your new couch or dinette set. It means you have a problem, that you need to get the roof fixed and it will cost you money to get it fixed. The hole in the tree house roof was not a problem — it was an adventure.

Me: I agree with all You have said, and I notice that it applies to my own children. I think what I am doing is more important than what they are doing because I can be more serious about it or perhaps because it brings in the all-important money. No, I guess the money part doesn't hold up because I sometimes take what is supposed to be recreation more seriously than I take my job.

I tell my children that I cannot be bothered with their games, and when they ask me what I am doing, I tell them that I don't have time; I am too busy to explain. When I make time for the children, I often make frantic attempts at entertainment, like taking them to Disney World, when sitting together in the back yard or reading a book would please them endlessly. Isn't it ironic that I say I have to work hard to buy my kids what they want when, in fact, all they want is me— and I'm not available for them while I'm at work? **I deprive them of me to give them what they don't want.**

God: Yes. It is funny in a sick sort of way. All they want is you, but they have given up having you. Your children attempt to replace having you by giving you justification to work; so they continue their constant requests for Ninja Turtles or the GI Joe with the Kung Fu grip. If you wondered why you never cared much for those toys, it is because they are a hollow replacement for you.

Me: Since our conversations began, I have noticed myself spending more time with my kids and doing less while I am with them. I have discovered that we don't always have to be doing something.

God: Congratulations. You can learn a lot from your kids — before you teach them anything. Once you have taught them, then you can only learn from them what you have taught them. The more time you spend with your children, the better, but make it time without structure — **free time as opposed to quality time.** Your children are **always** learning **everything** from you.

Me: I will spend more time with my kids. I am also spending more time with my spouse. When our fights don't last as long, we get to spend more time together without there even being more time.

God: Time spent acting out a script or running a routine, like you described with the fight patterns with your spouse, doesn't count as time at all. As long as you are going to have the illusion of time, you may as well have as much of it as you can. The easiest way I know of to do that is for you to have very few routines and habits. **Routines and habits are viruses that feed on time.** Before you know it, they will eat up all your time, and there will be none left.

Me: I do notice that since we have been talking, I have more time, so I guess time is not as absolute as I thought. Clocks are not flexible enough to measure time. If we are flexible enough, we can measure time accurately, and destroy it and create it as well.

God: Now you are talking.

Me: I have to go now. I am late for an important appointment.

God: What?

Me: Just kidding. I lose time, gain time and can joke about time all at the same time.

God: I get it. Funny. (God laughs)

Me: I think when we started these conversations I would have thought an appointment could be more important than talking with You or taking care of myself or celebrating. I have come a long way, and not moved at all. I had better watch out—I am starting to talk like You.

God: You can tell a lot about people by the company they keep. Being around me probably won't do you any harm.

Me: That is an understatement. You have taught me more about priorities than I have ever known without even talking about them. You have taught me so much, and I will show You what I have learned by how I live.

God: Yes, you will. You can't help but show me, and if you pay attention, you will discover that you show yourself as well. I will leave you today (though I never leave). You will cease to be as aware of me as I give you a new and useful definition of Social Security.

Social Security is spending time around wonderful people.

Me: I have been doing a lot of that since I met You. Good-bye.

11

A t eleven months, Emily was walking, and her babbling was sounding more like talking. I suspected that as she learned to speak for herself, God would stop speaking to me. I so totally enjoyed our talks that it was hard to think of them ending. As language, consciousness and other distinctions reveal themselves to Emily she must forget that she knows everything and begin to accumulate what she can learn. I was at a different point in the cycle — ready to delight in everything once again. I still didn't know whether I believed in God; it didn't seem to matter. I had learned so much, and it was this very process of learning that led me to this point.

I realized that God's conversations with me were almost over and that there was not much left to say, perhaps there never had been. While standing beside Emily's bed and listening to her breathing, I initiated our last conversation.

Me: It has become obvious to me that we are going to stop meeting like this. Emily is developing a personality of her own.

God: Yes we are and yes she is. I have maintained the illusion that I am separate from you so that we could talk, and I am almost done doing so.

Me: You have left me to talk to me through my daughter, and You will be returning to me soon?

God: Yes. I won't maintain illusion for long, but I do so in special cases.

Me: You did in my case because I needed it?

God: No, I did in your case because you didn't. If people need me, I don't help them because they cannot use what I have to offer. I appear to people when they don't need help — so here I am.

Me: What You are saying doesn't sound like what I learned in Sunday School.

God: It isn't. I have never attempted to edit what I say to fit in the boxes you build for me. You can never build a box big enough to hold me, but it won't hurt you to keep trying. Problems occur when you stop building bigger boxes; then you miss so much.

Me: I want desperately to thank You for all You have done for me, but I know that the way I can show my appreciation is in the way I live. I don't need to say good-bye because You are not going anywhere, just everywhere. I may miss You, but only in my illusion. I can't help but find You if I attend to reality. I have two more questions for You. The first is: Do You exist?

God: I don't know.

Me: That doesn't sound like a "good" answer, but I suppose it is the one I am going to get.

God: It is **not** the one you are going to get, it is the one you **did** get. I may just as well ask you: Do I exist?

Me: I would have to say "Yes," but the moment that I say it, my mind comes up with evidence that You don't exist—even though we have been talking.

God: You understand the dilemma. It does not matter whether I exist or not. That is not a relevant question to me, and it is certainly only relevant to you theoretically. I have spoken to you of things that are practical. It is application and not knowledge that I am interested in for you.

Me: Thank You. I don't even remember my second question. It seems amazing to me that we have talked so much and avoided the usual religious or spiritual words. We have not talked about Jesus, will, spirit, Christianity, the Buddha, Mass, heaven, hell, holiness or any number of other terms that would usually come up in such a conversation. Thanks for avoiding all of these words. They seem to confuse the issue because everyone who uses them means something different by them. In parting (this parting without parting), thanks for everything. I continue to discover that I am more a part of You and You are more a part of me than I can ever know. I feel it. I feel it **All**.

God: You are welcome. I will leave you (return to you) with a joke.

There were three construction workers. They were taking their lunch break at the top of a twenty-story building. As they opened their lunch boxes, the first worker said, "Not bologna again. I can't take this. Every day a bologna sandwich." (Like so many people on Earth, his anger masks fear, but the anger is so close to the surface that it is waiting to come out at the simplest and most unimportant thing.) "I can't stand another day with bologna." The next day the same thing happens, and the next and the next. A week goes by, and every day the construction worker has a bologna sandwich in his lunch box. Finally he says, "One more day with bologna and I jump. I just can't stand it anymore."

The other two construction workers are a little nervous the next day as lunch time nears. They sit down to lunch. The first worker opens his lunch box to discover another bologna sandwich, and he jumps the twenty stories to his death. The second worker says, "Isn't that awful? I can't believe he actually jumped."

The third worker says, "What are you so upset about? He makes his own lunch."

Have fun, play, and I will be watching you. I will be with you. Now it is your turn to tell me a story.

Me: The other day when my wife and I had our short fight and our good laugh, Judson said he didn't like it when we fought, even though it was very seldom. He went on to explain that when we fight, he goes to his own apartment called happiness.

Early one morning I attempted to show Judson where the big dipper was. It didn't go very well. **It is difficult to point out an illusionary shape from a great distance.** He did not see it. Not one to quit, I continued to point it out to him. Finally he said, "Oh, you mean the big question mark?"

I had been taught to see the big dipper. Judson taught me to see the big question mark. I wonder what the same constellation looks like from your, every, perspective. It is a pleasure to be curious. I live in wonder at the mysteries of life, knowing full well that they are only mysteries from my perspective. There is something so natural about adopting different perspectives. It is entertaining without effort, and it doesn't cost anything but my limitations.

My son also said that Mother Nature is Your wife. Is that true?

God: Could be. There is a lot you can learn from your children, not the least of which is the ability to have constant insights and brilliant thoughts without holding on to them. Now get back to your play.

Me: Thank You. Good-bye and hello.

God: YES.

The next day Emily spoke for the first time, and now, five years later, she hardly stops talking. Emily must learn and grow at her pace. I interfere as little as possible. I seek to be a model for her, which is easy because what is best for me is best for her also. I still talk to God, but I can no longer hear God speaking with me directly.

Epilogue

Can you believe in God? Can you not believe in God? When I started this book I neither believed or didn't believe, I was impartial. More than that, I considered believing or not believing in God to be irrelevant.

Somewhere in the editing process, I began to believe in God (I don't think that it was due to editing). I don't believe in God based on evidence. I see miracles everyday: watching my son or daughter, sitting in the hot tub on a 0 degree day with the sun shining and the bright blue sky overhead, smelling a campfire or tasting my wife's fresh apple pie. I could go on, but I think you get the idea. The list is infinite. **I won't impose on all of these miracles the proof of a deity.**

I have discovered that I need no proof to believe in God. I can believe if I enjoy believing. I can believe when I get the least bit lonely in this huge universe. I not only can believe — I do believe. I don't claim that there is a God — the existence of God is a controversy I have no interest in. Belief and truth are unrelated and may as well remain that way.

It's fun, it's pleasant and it just might be useful to believe in God. There is no particular form to my belief. There is just a new warmth within me. I have lost loneliness and fear and gained all other possibilities.

As I write this, Emily is a happy and healthy six year old going on fifteen. Would I prefer to have Emily than God — what is the difference?

Some Play

A little bit of practice goes a long way. Here are some exercises that will lighten you up and encourage you to have more fun.

• Look up. Literally. Chances are anytime you are upset you are either looking down and to your right or down and to your left.

• Add novelty to your life by varying the way you do some of your repetitious behaviors.

• Learn to watch or hear your thoughts rather than being your thoughts. Thoughts are for your entertainment.

• Dance for at least fifteen minutes per day.

• Eat more fruits and vegetables.

• Practice laughing. Encourage others to laugh by laughing more yourself.

• Spend a day doing nothing.

• Blow some bubbles outdoors. You can use dish soap or buy some bubble solution. Watch the bubbles. Chase the bubbles. Play.

About Jerry Stocking

Jerry Stocking is a modern day Thoreau living in the woods in Northern Wisconsin with his wife, Jackie, and children, Emily (6) and Judson (2). When he has something to write, Jerry commutes about forty feet from his house to his office. Jerry rises when he chooses (usually about 3:00 AM) and goes to bed when he wants to (usually about 10:00 PM.) His woods retreat has the latest computer equipment yet is unsoiled by television, alarm clocks, fast food or other vices so prevalent in the world. This atmosphere is conducive to the introspection so lacking in our fast-paced world. The children are living the freedom of being loved and cared for by two full-time parents and are being homeschooled.

Jerry hasn't always lived in the woods. He used to live in Milwaukee, WI and drive to work wearing a suit and tie. He was a successful financial consultant at Shearson Lehman Brothers. His past careers span the gamut of experience from owning his own retail stores to being an industrial designer to selling investments. All of Jerry's occupations have some things in common — he was successful at each of them and all of his job changes required a greater commitment to people and an increased ability to relate effectively with his clients and co-workers. Jerry loves people and is committed to finding out what is possible for "us" as human beings. His love of people and desire to contribute to them is apparent in his writing and lecturing.

Jerry is the president of a non-profit corporation, A Choice Experience, Inc., and a publishing company called Moose Ear Press. A Choice Experience, Inc. offers occasional workshops and a sixteen page quarterly newsletter, *Bridging the Gap,* which focuses on human possibility. The topics covered range from spirituality to personal growth to social commentary.

Jerry's credentials are impressive educationally, and even more so, experientially. A Master Practitioner of Neuro-Linguistic Programming (NLP), Jerry has been studying and using NLP for the past ten years. He has done extensive training in other-than-conscious communication and no-fault psychology. He graduated in 1974 from Northern Michigan University with degrees in psychology and philosophy. Though still learning and exploring daily Jerry has reached a point where he is ready to give back some of what he has learned in hopes that it will improve the quality of life for others.

Books by Jerry Stocking

Cognitive Harmony, An Adventure in Mental Fitness

There are No Accidents, A Magical Love Story

Introduction to Spiritual Harmony

Spiritual Harmony Vol. I

Spiritual Harmony Vol. II

Most people are mentally flabby. A few people are mentally fit. Mentally fit people produce more with less effort than their flabby counterparts. They enjoy life more and people want to be around them. They have better jobs and better relationships.

The book *Cognitive Harmony, An Adventure in Mental Fitness*, provides you with explanations and exercises in Mental Fitness.

Paul R. Sheele, MA, the chairman of Learning Strategies Corporation says, "*Jerry Stocking has taken a bold leap from analyzing behaviors and the structure of experience into describing the domain of consciousness. Delightfully, he has handled the leap adroitly. His blend of Neuro-Linguistic Programming and spiritual psychology gives personal growth aspirants a sturdy ladder to climb.*"

Hayward Allen of the Wisconsin State Journal says, "*The text is punctuated by drawings and a multitude of exercises to get into cognitive shape. This is definitely an introspective book. The reader is helped to develop expressiveness, perceptions and thinking patterns.*"

The sooner you begin reading *Cognitive Harmony, An Adventure in Mental Fitness*, the sooner you will be mentally fit and getting much more out of life.

Cognitive Harmony, An Adventure in Mental Fitness
$22.50 + $2.25 shipping and handling ($24.75)
Moose Ear Press   ISBN 0-9629593-0-8

Bridging The Gap

An Occasional Journal of Human Possibility
A Cognitive Harmony Publication

What Gap?
What you do......What you say
Everyday Struggle......Spirituality
Reality......Perception
You......Other People

This publication reaches out to people who want to be reminded to come out and play. Each issue is filled with stories, articles and insights from the Stocking home in Northern Wisconsin. Your subscription to Bridging the Gap will bring you four more issues as they come out—expect them to arrive when they do, rather than on a set timetable. We will use your contribution to A Choice Experience, Inc. to further and sustain our non-profit corporation, and to ensure lively reading for you over the next year.

Contact Moose Ear Press to find out about quantity discounts of *Introduction to Spiritual Harmony* or for information on other books and tapes by Jerry Stocking.

Moose Ear Press

PO Box 335
Chetek, WI 54728

715-924-4906
FAX 715-924-4738

Contact A Choice Experience, Inc. for information on our Bridging the Gap newsletter or seminars.

A Choice Experience, Inc.

PO Box 335
Chetek, WI 54728

715-924-4906
FAX 715-924-4738